DANCES OF THE OLDEN TIME.

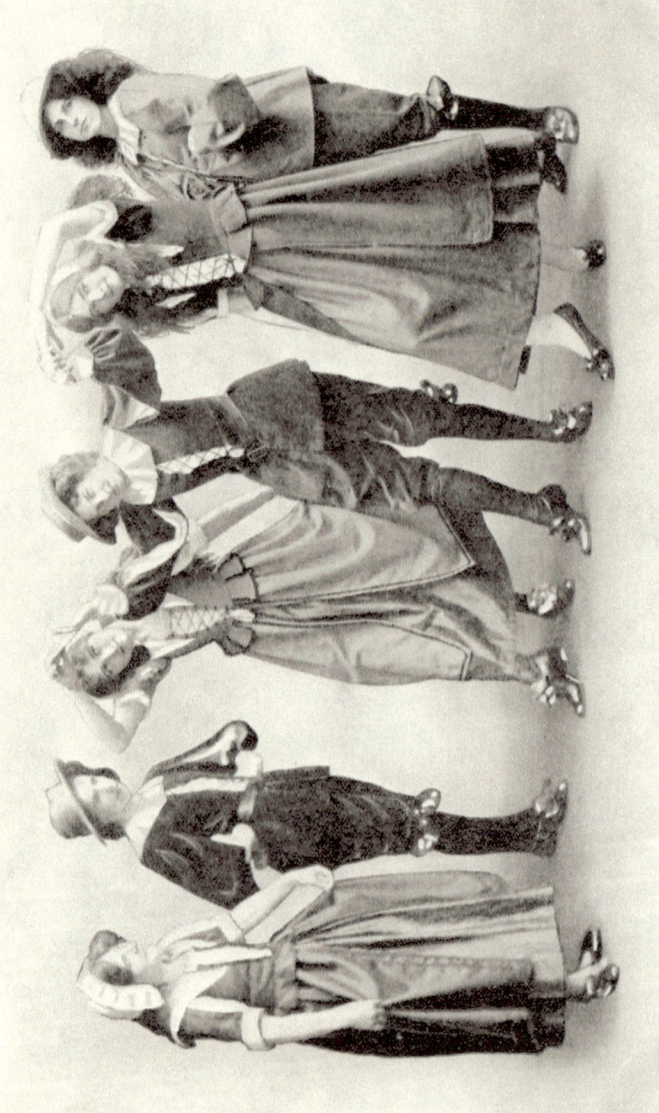

KEMP'S JIG

DANCES

OF THE

OLDEN TIME,

Arranged for the Pianoforte

BY

ALFRED MOFFAT.

*With an Essay on Old English Dancing, and the Method
explained of performing a number of Dances
included in this work*

BY

FRANK KIDSON.

CONTENTS.

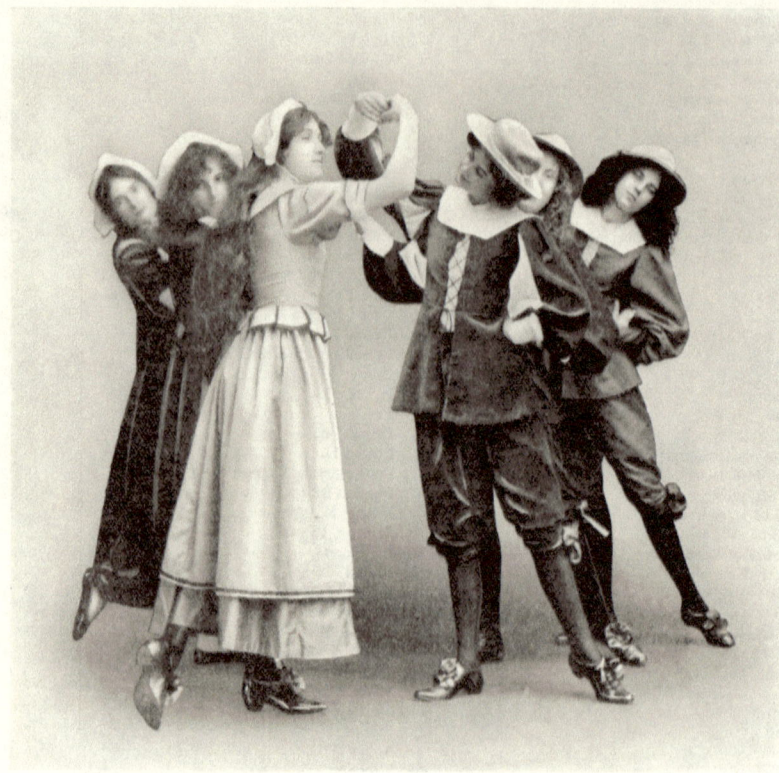

ALL IN A GARDEN GREEN

OLD ENGLISH DANCING

BY

FRANK KIDSON.

THE art of dancing as a social amusement has never lacked votaries in England, and there is sufficient evidence to show that, in bygone times, skill and grace went to its practice there fully as much as in nations that claim supremacy in the art.

To go no further back than Saxon times, there is a plenitude of reference and pictorial examples to show that the art was in esteem for private amusement, and that it was engaged in by professional exponents who had attained more than ordinary skill. Jugglers, posturers, gleemen, and dancers seem to have gone about in parties from village to village, or town to town, exhibiting their art much in the same way that teams of Morris dancers formerly travelled for the same purpose.

In Elizabeth's day, when peace fell more upon the land than it had in former years, rustic dancing appears to have had either a great revival, or greater notice was taken of the pastime. The Queen seems to have been more devoted to her people than previous monarchs, and in her reign Morris dancing and rustic sports met with official favour and recognition. The Robin Hood sports, which included archery contests, dancing round the Maypole, the hobby horse pranks, and Morris dancing, were a frequent recreation. The English country dance then probably got its name and took a more concrete form. The Morris dance, whatever be its origin (a question much disputed), had as a primal necessity the accompaniment of bells, which were worn on the knees and ankles of the men who performed it. Women were never rightly admitted to the Morris. It was properly confined to active young men who formed themselves into sets belonging to different villages, much in the same way as our present football teams are constituted, and they upheld the honour of their respective villages in contests of skill. Many villages had particular tunes associated with the dance, thus we get "Stanes' Morris" (see p. 10 of present volume), and other Morris tunes belonging to certain places are similarly existent.

THE HORNPIPE was originally an instrument formed of a cow's horn provided with a hollow piece of wood, or bone, pierced like a flute. The simple rustic tunes performed on this instrument were associated with the name, and they gradually settled into a distinct form of composition. Early hornpipes, composed before the middle of the 18th century, were tunes in triple time. After this period the hornpipe was generally written, in common time, and at a still later period the even quavers were frequently broken up into a dotted quaver and a semi-quaver, thus giving a sort of "snap" effect. The hornpipe dance as we know it is a step dance performed by a solo dancer. The hornpipe tunes, as well as jig tunes, were, however, frequently used in the ball room for country dances, and then had the usual country dance figures allotted to them.

THE JIG, like the Hornpipe, is named after an ancient instrument, which in this case was a small fiddle. The Jig as a dance is generally in 6-8 or 9-8 time, and is popular at the present day in Ireland. It is danced by a man and woman facing each other. They dance in recognised step, and perform some evolutions without contact with each other. It can hardly be questioned that the jig has formerly been a different dance from what is now practised under that name. It appears always to have been one in which much exertion was required, and it is possible that the Galliard was an original form of it.

"Kemp's Jig." published in the 17th century, was named after a certain Kemp, who in 1599 danced from London to Norwich in nine days. He wrote an account of this feat, and calls the dance a "Morris," but it was probably only a Morris in the sense that he had bells on his knees. The step was probably to a jig tune, and quite likely may have been the one printed at page 28 of present volume.

The Country Dance.

Chief among old English dances is the country dance. This retained favour for three or four centuries, and was only ousted from popular approval by the quadrille and the lancers, to which it has many points of similarity. In regard to its name it must be distinctly stated that it derives nothing from "Contra-danse," the French equivalent. This term is merely a foreign rendering of the English word, and is not to be taken as indicating the position of the dancers at the commencement—that is, opposite each other. Our English country dance was one originally performed by the English rustic people, afterwards becoming a favourite in the ball room, where it gave as much enjoyment as on the village green.

The primitive instinct with dancers, where no figures are provided, is to dance round an object. The object might be a captive, an altar, or other sacred emblem. Perhaps this altar or emblem might be decorated with a trophy taken from the enemy, and we may thus look upon the Maypole with its garlands and streamers as an embodiment of this emblem, and the dance round it as a survival of the primitive usage. The same tradition is also found in children's ring games, among which "Here we go round the mulberry bush" may be cited as an example.

Without pursuing further this aspect of the question, it may be stated that many early country dances are to be found named " Round, O," or " Rounds " (see present volume, page 29), and this style of dance survived for a considerable time. At a later date the circular variety gave place to other types, until finally the country dance settled down into the "long" form described more particularly further on.

Unlike other dances, the country dance is not confined to one particular set of evolutions. It may be very aptly described as something like chess play—that is, it obeys certain conventional movements, but the sequence of these movements differs in each dance, consequently each country dance only resembles another in general principle, but not in detail. Apart from the difficulty of learning the recognised figures, the frequenters of fashionable balls had to possess expert knowledge as to the method of dancing each dance then in favour. This meant that dancing country dances, to say nothing of the minuet and cotillion, was a business that required time, thought, and practice. To impart this knowledge was the professional business of a large army of dancing masters, who, scattered in London and the provinces, made a living by it. Many of these dancing masters visited country houses, and spent much time in teaching the dances to the family before the county balls. This was the general practice towards the end of the 18th century.

The first collection of country dances and their tunes was published in 1650 by John Playford, and was named " The English Dancing Master."

From the directions given in that work, and its many succeeding editions, it is evident that the country dance of the 17th century was very different from what it later became. In the present volume many tunes are reprinted from Playford's work, and I append the original directions as given by the author for several of the dances.

KEMP'S JIG (see page 28).—The dancers are limited to six, the men and women stand in a circle, the sexes being alternate.

" One man lead in two women forward and back. Honour to one, honour to the other, then turn the third. Lead your own with your left hand, and the woman you turned, and as much. Then as much with the other two women, turning your own. The next man as much. Then the third as much. (The next section of the dance.) First man lead the women as before, turn half round, holding both hands and his own, as much to the other, turn the third woman. Do thus to all, the rest following and doing the like. (Next section of the dance.) First man take the women as before by the couple, hands behind, then lead them forwards and back, pull one half about and kiss her, as much with the other, turn the third. Do thus to all, the rest following and doing the like."

TEN POUND LASS (see page 19). This dance is named as " longways for as many as will "— that is, the men and women stand opposite to each other.

" The first and second men lead through between the first and second women and turn single (a single is two steps closing both feet). Then the first and second women lead through the men and turn single. Then the first couple lead through the second, cast up and cast off, and so on."

TRENCHMORE (see page 30, " Longways for as many as will ").—" Lead up all a double (a double is four steps forward and backward, closing both feet) and back, cast off, meet below, and come up. Do so again. First couple go down under the second couple's arms, and the third couple come up under the first. Do this forward and back. (Next section of dance.) First man set to the second woman, then to his own, then to the third woman, then to his own, then to the fourth woman, then to his own, and so to all the women and men. Then your woman do the same. Then arm them as you set to them, arming your own, then your woman as much.

" (Next section.) Lead up again, then turn your woman with your right hand, and the second woman with your left, your woman following as you turn till you come to your place, then your woman do the same, you following her, the rest doing these changes."

Quaint as the language is, the reader will probably be able to follow these directions and apply them to the music.

The Helston Furry Dance.

This is a curious survival of a custom, thought to be part of a pagan rite which is still practised at Helston, in Cornwall. On old May day—the 8th of May—the inhabitants join hands in couples and dance through every house in the village, singing doggerel words to the tune given on page 50 of the present work. The object is to bring good luck to every house which the dancers enter. There are other festivities in connection with the dancing, and the custom as at present followed dates back to a remote past. The tune has evidently been a Morris dance, and what may be accepted as its original form is printed at page 22.

There is no space to discuss the origin of the dance or to tell in full the different theories which have been put forth in explanation of the strange custom, a custom, moreover, which holds no place in our English folk lore save at Helston.

Foreign Dances Popular in England.

THE PAVAN.—A time came when the simple dances of the English people were considered either vulgar, out of date, or lacking in grace. Intercourse with foreign countries became more general, and those who had made Continental tours and stayed at foreign courts brought over new dances to supersede the more common-place English ones. In the middle of the 16th century the Itailan influence on all arts and amusements was greatly felt, and Italian music and dances were thought to be much superior to our own native productions. It was then that such dances as the Pavan, the Galliard, and the Coranto came to England. The Pavan was probably a native Italian dance, although there was also a Spanish form of it.

The origin of the word " Pavan " is a matter of doubt. Some derive it from Padua, where the dance was supposed either to have had its origin or to have been in great favour. Others say that the word comes from " pavo "—a peacock. The gorgeous trains of the ladies and the strutting and display of fine garments favour this notion of its derivation.

However this may be, the fact remains that the dance was one of state and ceremony, and its chief design appears to have been the exhibition of courtly grace, and the display of costly robes, the ladies having heavy trains, sometimes held up by pages, or ladies-in-waiting.

The steps of the Pavan are described by Jean Tabourot, a French monk, who under the assumed name of Thornot Arbeau published a work on dancing in 1588. From this it appears that the Pavan is a " couple " dance, and that while several couples may be engaged in the dance at the same time they dance without reference to each other saving, of course, that each couple is dancing to, and keeping perfect time with, the same music. The lady and gentleman take hold of hands, and there is much bowing and curtseying, as in the later minuet. They execute graceful movements, and the steps partake more of a walking than a dancing or skipping character. The Pavan seems to have suggested many other dances that were current long after the dis-appearance of the original. The Gavotte and the Minuet may be cited as probable successors to the Pavan.

Like other dances the Pavan became a musical form for composers, and there are numerous compositions entitled Pavans scat-tered through early manuscript volumes of music. The Fitzwilliam Virginal book (early 17th century) contains many which were pro-bably never intended to be used for dancing, but merely as instrumental works to be played on the Virginals. The Pavan was in either two-four time or common time, and as befitted its stately character was of a slow movement.

In the latter part of the 16th century a popular Pavan tune called the " Spanish Pavan " was in great use, and many ballads of a doleful cast were adapted to it.

THE GALLIARD.—The Galliard was a brisk and lively dance which seems to have been danced immediately after the stately Pavan. Its chief characteristics seem to have been jumping and skipping, and probably a certain amount of latitude was given to the dancers to display individual agility.

An early mention of the Galliard occurs in Piers Plowman, and it incidentally shows that dancing schools were held in taverns. The passage in modernised spelling runs thus :—

" Now was there one man of our company that was as deaf as a door nail. When we were come into the school, the musicians were playing, and one dancing of a Galliard, and even at our entry he was beginning a trick as I remember of sixteens or seven-teens. I do not very well remember, but wonderfully he leaped, flung, and took on, which the deaf man beholding, and not hearing any noise of the music, thought verily that he had been stark mad and out of his wits, and of pure pity and com-passion ran to him and caught him in his arms and held him hard. The dancer not knowing his good meaning, and taking it to the worst, drew his dagger, and smote the man on the head very sore."

The Galliard is described by an old writer, Sir John Davis, as " a swift and wandering dance, with lofty turns and capriols in the air."

It appears that the dance was not always the gay madcap frisk that it afterwards degene-rated into, for Arbeau says of it (1588) that formerly when the dancer had taken his partner for the Galliard, they first placed themselves at the end of the room, and after a bow and curtsey, walked once or twice round it. Then the lady danced to the other end of the room, and remained there dancing while the gentleman following presented himself before her, made some steps, and then turned to the right and left. After that she danced to the other end, and he followed doing some steps, and so on again and again. " But now," says Arbeau, " in towns they dance it tumultuously, and content themselves with making the five steps and some movements without any design, caring only to be in position on the sixth of the bar.

In the first four steps the left and right feet of the dancer were raised alternately, and on the fifth of the bar he sprung into the air, twisting round and capering as best he could; the repose on the sixth note gave more time for a lofty spring."

Burton, in his "Anatomy of Melancholy," speaking of the dancing of a Galliard, says:— "Let them take their pleasures, young men and maids, flowering in their age, fair and lovely to behold, well attired, of comely carriage, dancing a Greek Galliarde, and, as their dance requires, keep their time, now turning, now tracing, now apart, now together, now a curtsey, then a caper, etc.; it is a pleasant sight."

Thomas Morley, in his "Plaine and easie Introduction to Practical Musick," 1597, refers to Pavans and Galliards as follows (modern spelling):—

"After every Pavan we usually set a Galliard (that is a kind of music made out of the other, causing it to go by measure, consisting of a long and a short stroke successively. This is a lighter and more stirring kind of dancing than the Pavan, consisting of the same number of strains. The Italians made their Galliards, which they term 'Salta-relly' plain, and frame ditties to them, which in their masquerades they sing and dance, and many times without any instrument at all."

Morley, above, refers to the Italians setting songs to the Galliard tunes, the English also followed the same fashion. "The Frogs' Galliard" was used for the song, "Now, O now, I needs must part," and "Wigmore's Galliard" had also a song adapted to it. In an early play one of the characters is made to say: "This will make my master leap out of bed for joy, and dance 'Wigmore's Galliard' in his shirt about his chamber."

The Galliard was in triple or compound triple time. It has been said that was the same as the "Cinque pace," but Chappell points out that while the Galliard is in a triple, the cinque pace is in common time, the fifth step coming upon the first note of the succeeding bar.

Partly associated with the Galliard was the "Brangle," or "Branle," or "Brawle." This was a wild kind of dance, and some say it owes the name "Brawl" to the appearance it gave to a street scuffle. This is doubtless a far-fetched conclusion. The dancers, it is believed, took hands and danced round in a ring. It was a French dance in common time, and there was more than one variety of it.

THE ALMAN, ALMAIN, or ALLEMANDE is said, as its name indicates, to have originated in Germany. Of it Morley says:—

"The Alman is a more heavy dance than this (the Galliard), fitly representing the nature of the people whose name it carrieth, so that no extraordinary motions are used in dancing of it. It is made of strains, sometimes two, sometimes three, and every strain is made by four, but you must mark that the four of the Pavan measure is in duple proportion to the four of the Alman measure," etc.

This, of course, means that the Almain is in common time. The English country dance retains a figure called "Allemande," which is, doubtless, a survival of one part of the original Almain figure. In the country dance it is a circular back to back figure.

THE CANARIES is a dance to which but scant reference is found.

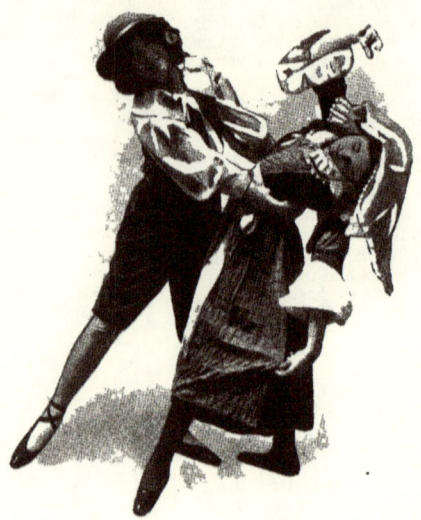

THE TAMBOURIN.

It seems to have been imported from the Canary Islands during the reign of Elizabeth, but probably never became really very popular. Shakespeare refers to it in "Love's Labour Lost," and a copy of the tune is given by Arbeau. It is said to have been danced in Spain, and perhaps originated in a ballet or a masque, for there was one connnected with the dance in which the performers were habited as Kings and Queens of Morocco, or as savages.

This is given as the figure danced:—

Lady and gentleman dance together, and then pass towards the end of the hall. He leaves her here, but returns and again retreats, always facing her. The lady then performs the same, and this is repeated several times, a variety of steps being used in the dance. The music was sometimes performed with the aid of castanets held by the dancers.

THE SARABAND was imported into England from Spain, or from a Spanish source, probably it may originally have belonged to the Moors. It was danced with castanets, and seems to have been a solo dance, or danced as the Irish Jig by two people who step it, facing each other, but independent in their movements. There are many references to the Saraband as early as Elizabeth's day.

THE PASSEPIED or PASPY.—This is a dance in triple time popular, in far off days, in Brittany. It is thought to be a variety of the Branle, but is said to resemble in some degree the Minuet.

THE CHACONE. —It is asserted that the dance got its name from "Ciacona," a blind man, as one so afflicted is said to have invented it. This statement may very reasonably be doubted. Grassineau in his *Musical Dictionary*, 1740, gives it as a "kind of dance in the air of a Saraband, derived from the Moors. The bass always consists of four notes which proceed in conjoint degrees wherein they make divers concords and couplets with the same burden." Grassineau further says that "the word is formed of the Italian Ciacona of Cecone, a blind man, this air being said to have been invented by such a one." The old spelling is frequently "Chacoon."

THE BOURRÉE.—It is popularly supposed that this French dance was a provincial peasant dance introduced from Auvergne by Catherine de Medicis in 1565. It appears to have had some degree of similarity to our English country dance, for the dancers begin by standing opposite each other. It is said to be still popular in Auvergne, where the peasants dance it with all vigour and pleasure.

They sing to the dance, and there are various steps employed in it. The music is in common or two-four time.

THE CORANTO or COURANTE.—This must originally have had a "running" figure, and is probably, as its name indicates, a native of France.

Morley (1597) says : "Like to this (the Branle), but more light to the Voltes and Courantes, which being both of a measure are, notwithstanding, danced after sundry fashions. The Volte rising and leaping, the Courante traversing and running. The Courante hath twice so much in a train as the English country dance."

Arbeau (1588) speaks of it as having in his youth been danced thus :— Three young men and three young girls stand all in a row. The first man led his lady to the far end of the room, and left her there while he returns to the others. The two other men do the same, until the ladies and men are at different ends of the room. The men in turn advance to the ladies, who in gesture repel them by a wave of the hand. The men evince despair, and approach more humbly, and ultimately the ladies are conquered, and allow the male dancers to dance out Courante with arms round waists. This is

THE BOURRÉE.

obviously a sort of pantomimic dance, and probably was modified when it got into the ball room. The Courante was in triple time.

THE RIGADOON.—Grassineau (1740) says that the dance came from Provence, is performed by a man and a woman, and is a gay and pleasant one. It was current in France in the time of Louis XIII., and according to Rousseau, took its name from one Rigaud, its inventor, or, more likely, one who brought it into notice. It was danced with a springing or jumping step, and is in common or two-four time. It became popular in England during the latter part of the 17th century.

THE MINUET or MENUET.—This was one of the most important of the 18th century dances. It is believed to have been introduced into Paris in 1650, and it is said that Louis XIV. danced it in public.

It is a stately " couple " dance, and performed with great dignity by the different couples who join in it. It is really a walking dance, but the walk must be a " step," and many curtseys and bows are exchanged between the lady and gentleman who constitute the couple.

In the 18th century it invariably opened the ball, the leading couple being the most distinguished lady and gentleman present. The gentleman wore his hat and sword, and the management of the former when he doffed it to make his bow to the lady, and the method of giving the hand and holding the skirt, on the

hands as they advance during the progress of the dance.

It is correctly in two-four time, though sometimes placed by the musician in common time.

THE COTILLION or COTILLON is a French dance, the word meaning a petticoat or a short skirt. It is quite evident that the modern Cotillion has little in common with the older form as danced in France and in England in the 18th century. In the latter case eight people joined in to form the dance—four ladies and four gentlemen. They formed a square, lady and gentleman being alternate, the partner being at the side. In arrangement it had much the form of the modern quadrille, and while couples " figured " independently of the rest, yet all occasionally combined in a figure. The

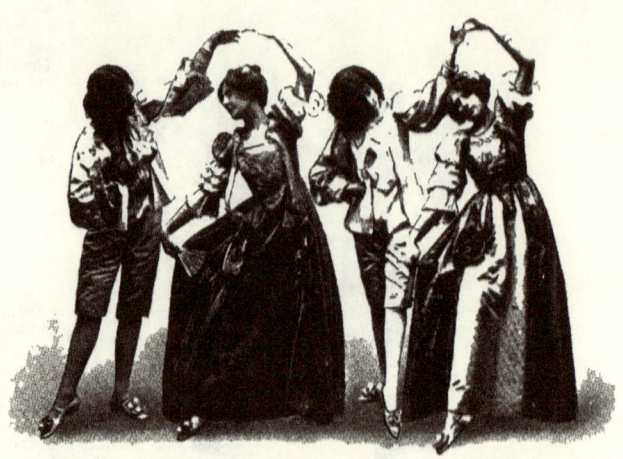

THE MINUET.

lady's part, were acts of graceful pose which were not to be easily acquired. The music is in triple time.

THE GAVOTTE.—This was originally a French peasant dance, and the manner of dancing it has changed considerably. It is said to have come from Gap in Dauphine, whose people are called " gavots." It is danced by a series of couples, one of which takes the lead holding and taking

modern Cotillion is much of a " go-as-you-please " set of figures, requiring toys as accessories and much romping, besides a number of absurd tricks planned beforehand.

THE MUSETTE and THE TAMBOURIN take their names from the instruments which provided the music, the bagpipe (musette) and the tambourine.

The Method of Dancing the Country Dance.

I have said that the country dance has changed very considerably during the time of its usage. In the 17th and early 18th centuries there were many figures and movements which were later discontinued. It had not then the regularity and system that it finally attained towards the end of the 18th century.

About this period it settled into two forms—the " whole set " and the " minor set." The principal feature of the whole set was that the top couple became the bottom couple at the end of each round of the tune ; the next, or second couple, began the next round, going at its conclusion below the original top couple, and so on until the original top couple came into action again. This form of the dance was soon found to be tiresome, if there were many couples, as only the top couple, or sometimes the second couple as its aid, were dancing, the rest remaining onlookers until their turn came round. The length too of the line of dancers made leading down the middle a scramble rather than a graceful movement. The " minor set " obviated this by making the dance consist of sets of three couples, so that thirty couples would make ten minor sets.

The bottom of the dance was then, not at the foot of the whole row, but merely below the third couple. The end of the first round brought the top couple into the second couple's place, the second round brought them into the third couple's position, and the third round made them the top couple of the minor set, and so until the original top couple had " gone down " the entire line of dancers. As soon as the original top couple had become the top couple of the second minor set. the original second couple commenced to dance as a top couple, and after the original top couple had passed down as top couple to a succeeding minor set, the minor set above it began as top couple, all dancing simultaneously, though the lower half of the dance remained inactive until the original leading couple had become top couple of the last of the minor sets.

This arrangement was probably not very satisfactory in practice, as it compelled the first leading couple to dance in excess, and the lowest couples might have to remain stationary during the whole period of the dance.

To get over this difficulty it was found best to make up a country dance into sets of three couples, each independent of the other, each set, where the length of the room permitted, dancing at the same time. The progression of couples from top to bottom was then merely confined to its own set of couples, avoiding thus the entanglements and mistakes that were always happening when minor sets were part of the general set.

The country dances figured in this work are taken from the old directions, and may be danced in the way just described—that is, in separate sets of three couples, and where there may only be four or even five couples dancing it will be found quite easy to adapt the figure so as to bring the top couple to the bottom, and not merely to below the third couple. As the top couple goes downward, the second and the third couples move upwards at the proper moment, the second couple becoming top couple, and the third the second couple, while the original " leading " or top couple becomes the third, and at the fourth time of playing the tune becomes top couple again. If there are four or five couples instead of three, it will, of course, be the fifth or sixth time of playing before the original top couple resumes its original position.

The Steps.

The steps of the country dance were deemed a matter of great importance, and to do the dance neatly it is as well to pay some attention to this part of it. It is obvious that the steps can only be learned from a teacher of dancing, and by much practice. In the present style of dancing it will be found the more practical way, in the country dance, to use the same steps that a good dancer employs in the modern Lancers. Though probably the stern old dancing masters of the 18th century would not have sanctioned so loose a rendering of a complicated business.

The Position of the Dancers.

The dancers stand facing each other at the commencement of the dance. The ladies on one side, the gentlemen facing them. Those opposite each other are partners. The " top " or " leading " couple. as it is indifferently called, is that which begins the dance, and is placed at that end of the room on the right hand of the ladies and the left of the gentlemen. Thus :—

(*Note*.—The gentlemen are the odd numbers—1, 3, 5—and the ladies the even numbers—2, 4, 6—throughout these diagrams.)

	2	4	6—Ladies.
Top			
	1	3	5—Gentlemen.

The lines of dancers should be about five feet apart, and the distance from each dancer at the side, about 2 feet 6 inches or 3 feet. The lines should be kept parallel as much as possible, and the dance performed with care, and without "romping." The music should be played evenly, and until the dancers have got to know the necessary evolutions, slowly. Anything like a scramble is fatal to the beauty of a country dance.

The music should be first played over by the musicians, and the dance commenced with a bow by the gentlemen and a curtsey by the ladies.

The Figures.

The figures in old country dances were many and complex. So complicated and grotesque were some that they gradually dropped out of fashion.

Among the principal ones in use at the end of the 18th century are the following :—

Lead down the middle.—The top or "leading" couple take hands—lady's right and gentleman's left—and dance down to bottom of line of dancers ; in these directions to below the third couple. This takes two bars.

Lead up is precisely the same going upwards—two bars. (The hands are changed at bottom—lady's left and gentleman's right.)

"*Cast-off*" or "*Cast-down*."—The lady and gentleman of the top couple make a short circuit upwards (two bars) and pass down behind their respective line of dancers—two bars more, four bars in all. (See diagram.)

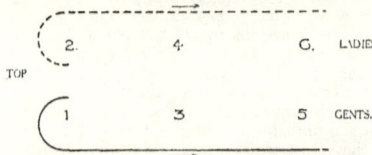

"*Cast-up*" is precisely the same figure as "cast-down," only the couple goes upwards. When the direction "cast-up" or "cast-down" is only given, it must be understood to mean that the top couple alone does it.

Turn.—Lady and gentleman join both hands and turn completely round from left to right—four bars of music. It may be performed by the couple each giving the right hand, the lady facing one way, the gentleman the other. In reversing the left hand is given.

Hands four round.—The first and second ladies join hands, the gentlemen do the same. The top gentleman joins with the top lady, and the second gentleman with the second lady. They move completely round from left to right—four bars of music. They can reverse, also four bars.

Hands six round.—The top and the third couple join hands, the second lady joins with the top and third lady, and the second gentleman with the top and third gentleman. They all move round in a circle left to right to their original positions—eight bars of music.

Hands across.—The top gentleman with the right hand takes the right hand of the second lady. The top lady in like manner takes the right hand of the second gentleman. The top gentleman and the second lady must have their hands uppermost, the other two hands being below theirs ; they turn completely round from right to left, taking four bars of music.

Allemande.—The top couple move in a complete circle round each other, back to back, returning to their places, each moving round towards their left hand.

"*Hey.*"—The "Hey" has many varieties ; it is a serpentine figure in which the dancer threads in and out the line of dancers. The "Heys" used in these directions are explained in the text.

Set.—In old books also called "Foot-it." It is practically the same with "Set to partners" in the modern Quadrille or Lancers. The lady and gentleman move cross corner ways to their right hands and bow, then to their left, bowing again. This should take four bars of music (two bars each way). Sometimes the lady, or the gentleman, alone does the setting. There is also a quicker "Set," which takes two bars. Plenty of space is required for "setting," and it must be done with deliberation and grace.

GENERAL OBSERVATIONS TO BE WELL NOTED.

It must be understood that throughout these directions the "top couple," or the "second," or "third" couple are those which stood in such positions at the commencement of the dance, although these positions may have changed during its evolution, and the "top couple" may be the second or third one in reality. The "bottom couple" is, in these directions, the third couple.

The partners in a country dance are the lady and gentleman who face each other.

The dance begins with the music being first played over, and just before the dance com-

mences the line of ladies and gentlemen curtsey and bow to each other. This is also done when the dance is finished, but not after each round of the tune.

The "passive couples" who are not moving during the time the top couple is dancing must be very alert to give room to the dancing couple, and to move upwards or downwards as may be required. They must quietly move upwards and take the place of the couple originally above them and the original second couple must be quick to perform the part of the original top couple the moment the first round of music is holding both hands they turn completely round (four bars). Then top lady, holding top gentleman's left hand in her right, they pass down to below third couple (two bars). Then up again to their places at top (two bars). Set to each other (four bars). Lead down the middle to bottom (two bars). Half set to each other (two bars). Allemande (four bars.)

ASH WEDNESDAY (see page 9).
Country Dance Figure.

First strain (once).—Top gentleman passes behind and below the second gentleman, and the second lady passes upward behind the top lady (four bars) ; she and the top gentleman meet in the centre and turn to their proper places (four bars).

First strain repeated.—The top lady and the second gentleman do the same figure.

Second strain.—The top couple join hands and lead down the middle, then up again (four bars). Allemande (four bars).

Second strain repeated.—The top lady and third gentleman meet in the centre and turn (four bars). Then the top gentleman and the third lady do the same figure (four bars). In turning, the top lady and the top gentleman take their places at the bottom, while the third couple occupy the second couple's place who have moved upward.

THE GIMCRACK (see page 13).

First strain.—Top couple cross over to opposite sides, taking position between the second and third couple, passing behind them, leaving lady and gentleman on their wrong sides (four bars). They set to each other (four bars).

First strain repeated.—Original top couple again cross over below the third couple, which brings them to their right sides (four bars). They turn (four bars).

Second strain.—The original top couple " Hey up "—that is, they pass behind third lady and third gentleman, and in front of the second lady and gentlmen, simultaneously to the top (four bars). Hands across with second couple (four bars).

Second strain repeated.—Top couple allemande (four bars). Top couple advance and retire (two bars). Then lead down to bottom of dance, taking the third couple's place (two bars).

PEACE AND PLENTY (see page 15).
Country Dance Figure.

First strain.—Top couple pass behind and round second couple (lady round lady, gentleman round gentleman), meet in centre and lead up hand in hand (four bars).

First strain repeated.—Top couple lead down middle and up again.

Second strain.—Top couple allemande.

Second strain repeated.—Top couple meet bottom couple in centre. Hands round and the bottom couple takes the place of the second couple, who move upward, while the original top couple takes the place of the third.

THE HAYMAKERS (see page 17).

First strain.—Top lady sets to second gentleman (four bars).

First strain repeated.—Top gentleman sets to second lady (four bars).

Second strain.—Hands across, first and second couples (four bars).

Second strain repeated.—Hands across the reverse way (four bars).

Third strain.—Top couple allemande (four bars).

Third strain repeated.—Top couple cast off behind dancers to bottom.

Note.—This is one of many ways of dancing " The Haymakers."

THE BALL (see page 22).

First strain.—Top couple set to each other (four bars), and then set to bottom corner partners (four bars).

First strain repeated.—Hands across by the top and second couples (four bars). Then change hands and go reverse way round (four bars).

Second strain.—Top couple go down the middle and up again (four bars). Turn at the top (four bars).

Second strain repeated.—Top couple cast off to bottom (four bars) and turn partners.

KISS ME EARLY (see page 33).

First strain.—Top couple set (four bars). Then turn (four bars).

First strain repeated.—Top couple casts down to below third couple (four bars) and turns (four bars).

Second strain.—Top lady, now at bottom, passes behind and round the third gentleman to her place at bottom again (four bars). Then top gentleman does the same figure, passing behind and round the third lady to his place at bottom again (four bars). (See diagram.)

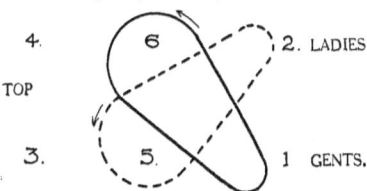

The lady and gentleman does this figure separately, *not* simultaneously. Top couple (at bottom) hands completely round with bottom couple (four bars), then allemande (four bars).

THE GOLD RING (see page 38).

Music played through (32 bars). Top and second couples set to partners (eight bars). Top lady crosses over below, and behind second gentleman, and into top gentleman's place. At the same time the top gentleman crosses below, and round the second lady into top lady's place (eight bars). Top couple (who are reversed in position) set to each other (eight bars), go back into their places by crossing back again in the same way they came (eight bars).

Music played through again (32 bars). Top gentleman turns top lady with one hand, leaving lady on gentleman's side (four bars). They meet again, and top gentleman turns lady into her place again (four bars). Then lead down the middle to below third couple and up again (eight bars). Allemande (eight bars). The top couple pass behind the second lady and second gentleman respectively, meet in middle, and lead down to bottom (eight bars).

HARLY BUSH FAIR (see page 42).

First strain.—First and second ladies, also first and second gentlemen, give a short set to each other (two bars). Then the two ladies join hands and cross over to the gentlemen's side. The first and second gentlemen pass on either side of them, leaving the centre passage to the ladies (two bars). The same figure, which brings them to their proper side again (four bars).

First strain repeated.—Top couple allemande (four bars). Top lady and top gentleman cross over, round, and behind second lady and second gentleman, taking the position held by the second couple, who move up.

Second strain.—The top couple (now in second couple's place) performs " whole figure," which is done thus (lady and gentleman moving simultaneously) :—

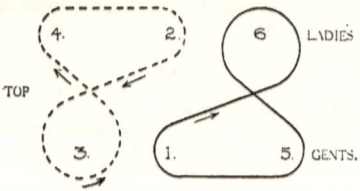

The lady at 2 moves in the direction of the arrow round the second gentleman (number 3), then crosses over behind the second lady (number 4) to her place in the middle. The top gentleman does the same figure (at the same time) round the third lady (number 6) and behind third gentleman (number 5) (eight bars). The original top lady and top gentleman cross over simultaneously to below the third couple, passing behind and round them (four bars). Top couple now turn and take the place of the third couple.

SIR ROGER DE COVERLEY (see page 49).

This time honoured dance, formerly known in Scotland as " The Maltman," dates from the middle of the 17th century. It has a figure which is distinctly its own, and it used to be performed as the " finishing dance " at all balls and assemblies. The figure has varied in the course of time, but the following is what may be called the " official " one, and is as danced in 1820.

The dancers are as many couples as can be mustered, placed facing each other as in the usual country dance ; ladies on one side, gentlemen on the other.

Top lady and bottom gentleman advance and meet in centre, and retreat to places.

Bottom lady meets top gentleman in centre and retreat to places.

Top lady and bottom gentleman meet in centre and turn with their *right* hands. Bottom lady and top gentleman do the same.

Top lady and bottom gentleman meet and turn with their *left* hands.

Bottom lady and top gentleman do the same. Top lady and bottom gentleman meet and turn with *both* hands.

Bottom lady and top gentleman do same. Top lady and bottom gentleman meet and allemande and retreat to places. Bottom lady and top gentleman do same.

Top couple make a serpentine figure thus :—

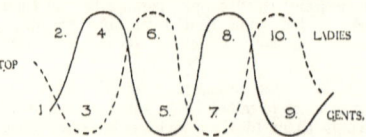

and meet at bottom. Should the set be long they may cross over every other couple, missing a couple each time. The top couple, now at the bottom, lead up the centre. The top lady " casts off " behind the ladies' line, the bottom couple take hands and pass upwards, and is followed behind by the next couple above them, and equally followed by the one above them and so on passing round the top lady's position until they regain their own places, except that the top lady is now at the bottom. This figure is sometimes done by the second couple following the top couple, but this reverses the position of the couples. The bottom couple then being at the top, whereas that is really the position of the second one, and it disturbs the sequence of the couples.

Sometimes the serpentine figure is converted into a " corkscrew figure," which is much more complicated and difficult to manage in time of the music.

DANNY (see page 54).

First strain.—Top lady crosses and goes below and round second gentleman, then round and behind second lady to her own place again at top (eight bars).

First strain repeated.—Top gentleman does the same figure, crossing below and behind second lady, back again behind second gentleman to his place again (eight bars).

Second strain.—Top couple allemande (four bars). Lead down middle and up again (four bars). Hands round with the second couple (four bars). Lead down the middle to below third couple (two bars). Top couple advance and retire (two bars).

WILL O' THE WISP (see page 56).

First strain.—Top couple lead down the middle and up again (eight bars).

First strain repeated.—Turn quite round with second couple (eight bars).

Second strain (16 bars).—The top couple cross over to below the third couple, round the third gentleman and third lady, and turn at the bottom until they are on their right sides, remaining in the place of the third couple, who move upwards (16 bars).

UP AND DOWN (see page 60).

First strain.—Top and second couple set to each other, lady to lady, gentleman to gentleman (two bars). Then change sides, ladies holding hands and passing through gentlemen (two bars). Then same figure repeated to bring back to places (four bars).

First strain repeated.—Top lady crosses and bows to second gentleman, then turns the bottom gentleman quite round and returns to place (four bars). (See diagram.)

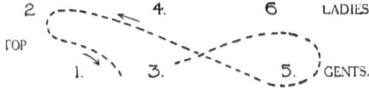

The top gentleman does exactly the same figure, crossing and bowing to the second lady, and turning the third lady, then back to place.

Second strain.—Top couple lead down middle and up again (four bars). Then top couple allemande.

Second strain repeated.—Top couple lead down the middle as far as second couple, then up again, separate at top, and cast down behind the dancers to the bottom, taking third couple's place (eight bars).

PEGGY PERKINS (see page 62).

First strain.—The ladies and gentlemen of the first and second couples set to each other simultaneously (four bars). Then the two couples set, the ladies join hands and cross over to gentlemen's side, the two gentlemen crossing to the ladies' side, one passing on each side of the ladies (four bars).

First strain repeated.—The same figure repeated, the couples thus getting to their original positions (eight bars).

Second strain.—Top couple lead down the middle and up again (four bars), and turn at top (four bars).

Second strain repeated.—The top couple cast off to below the third couple (four bars) and allemande (four bars).

KEW GREEN (see page 63).

First strain.—Top couple lead down to bottom and up again (four bars).

First strain repeated.—Top couple turn quite round (four bars).

Second strain.—Top lady crosses below and behind second gentleman, then to her place again. At the same time top gentleman does the same figure, crossing and passing round the second lady to his place again (four bars). Then advance and retire (two bars).

Second strain repeated.—Top couple set to each other at top (four bars). Then lead down the middle (two bars).

BELVEDIERE (see page 64).

Country Dance Figure.

First strain.—First lady sets to the second gentleman (eight bars).

First strain repeated.—First gentleman sets to the second lady (eight bars).

Second strain (eight bars).—Hands completely round with second couple (eight bars).

First strain again.—Top couple cast off behind dancers to the third couple's place.

THE MUFFIN (see page 65).

First strain.—Top couple allemande (four bars).

First strain repeated.—Top couple lead down the middle and up again (four bars).

Second strain.—Top couple set to each other (four bars). Then cast off to bottom, behind the dancers (four bars).

Second strain repeated.—Hands across completely round. Top couple, now at bottom, and third couple (four bars). Then right and left by top couple (now at bottom) thus.—Top couple passes completely round third gentleman and back to her place. Top gentleman does same figure round third lady (four bars). (*Note.*—The moving couple always keep to the right in passing.)

LA BELLE CATHERINE (see page 67).

First strain.—First gentleman sets to second lady (four brrs) and turns her (four bars).

First strain repeated.—First lady sets to second gentleman and they turn.

Second strain.—Top couple and second couple hands across (four bars). Then top couple lead down the middle and up again (four bars).

First strain once.—Top couple allemande (four bars). Then all six turn, leaving the top couple in the place of the third couple (four bars).

KITTY FISHER (see page 67).

First strain.—Top lady passes between second and third gentleman, round behind second gentleman to below third lady, round behind her and to bottom. The top gentleman does, at the same time, the same round the second lady and round the third gentleman (eight bars). (See diagram.)

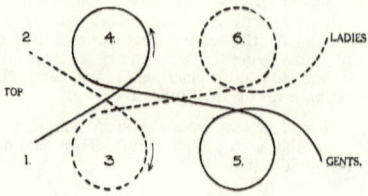

First strain repeated.—Top couple " Hey up " to top (four bars) and cast off to bottom (four bars).

Second strain.—Top couple set (four bars) and turn (four bars).

Second strain repeated.—" Hey up " from bottom (four bars) and cast down to bottom again (four bars).

Note.—To " Hey up " is thus :—Top lady passes behind third lady and in front of second lady to her place at top. Top gentleman does the same simultaneous y (four bars).

THE WEDDING RING (see page 68).

Country Dance Figure.

First strain.—Top couple set (four bars).

First strain repeated.—Top lady passess in front of second lady and behind third lady to bottom, and the top gentleman does the same on his own side, passing the gentleman. Top couple doing this movement simultaneously (four bars).

Second strain.—The top couple and the bottom couple join hands and turn round (four bars).

Second strain repeated.—They turn round the reverse way (four bars).

Third strain played twice.—The whole figure from the bottom—that is, top gentleman (from the bottom) passes in front of and behind the third lady, round the third gentleman, and behind him to his place at the bottom. The top lady does (at the same time) a similar movement, passing in front of and round the

third gentleman and up behind the third lady to her place at the bottom (eight bars). (See diagram.)

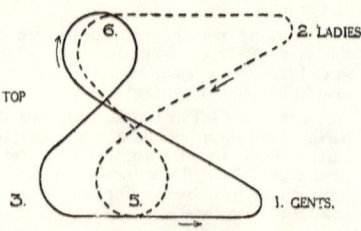

ALL IN A GARDEN GREEN (see page 21).

The following, put into more explanatory form, is Playford's directions for dancing to this tune, as given in the editions of the *Dancing Master*, 1650, etc.

First strain.—Three couples face each other, all advance to centre in four steps, then back again. All turn sideways, two steps to right ; then two steps to left.

First strain repeated.—Exactly the same figure.

Second strain.—Top gentleman shakes top lady by the hand, then the second and third ladies, the latter by one hand and then by the other. Kisses third lady twice and turns her.

Second strain repeated.—Top gentleman shakes third lady by the hand, then the second lady, then top lady, first by one hand and then by the other. Kisses her twice and turns her.

First strain repeated.—Top couple "set to partners," then all make two steps sideways, to the right and then to the left.

First strain repeated.—Same figure again.

Second strain.—The top lady shakes the top gentleman by the hand, then the second and third ladies, the latter first by one hand and then by the other. Kisses third gentleman and turns him.

Second strain repeated.—The top lady shakes third gentleman by the hand, then the second gentleman, then the top gentleman, first by one hand and then by the other. Kisses him twice and turns him.

First strain repeated.—The gentlemen link arms with each other and move two steps sideways, the ladies doing the same.

First strain repeated.—The same figure again.

Second strain repeated.—Top gentleman shakes top lady by the hand, then the second and third ladies, the latter one hand and then by the other. Kisses her twice and turns her.

Second strain again repeated.—Top gentleman shakes third lady by the hand, then the second lady, then the top lady, first by one and then by the other hand. Kisses her twice and turns her.

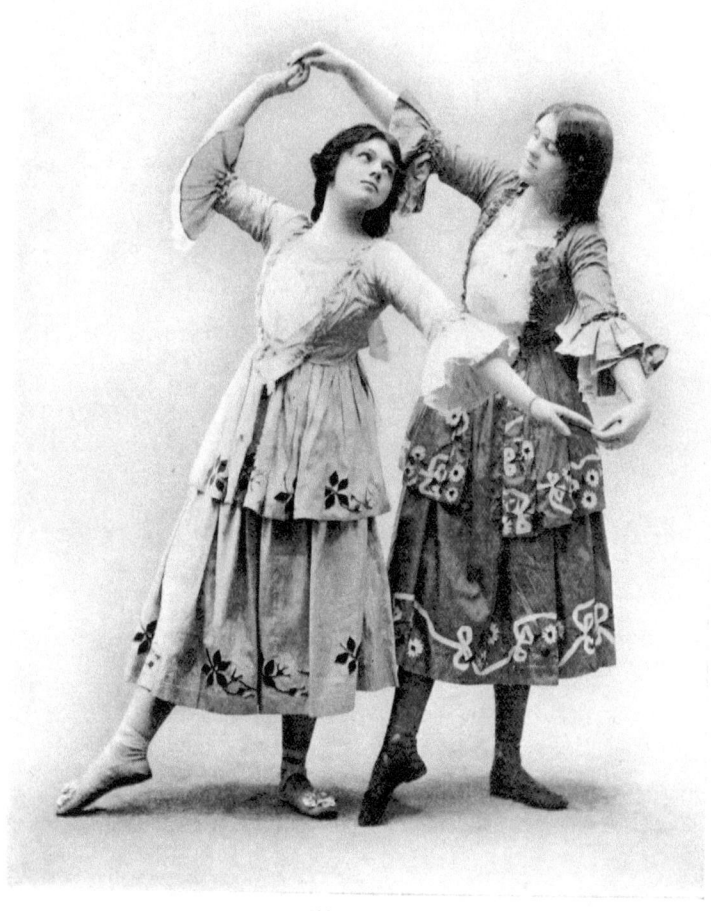

ALLEMANDE.

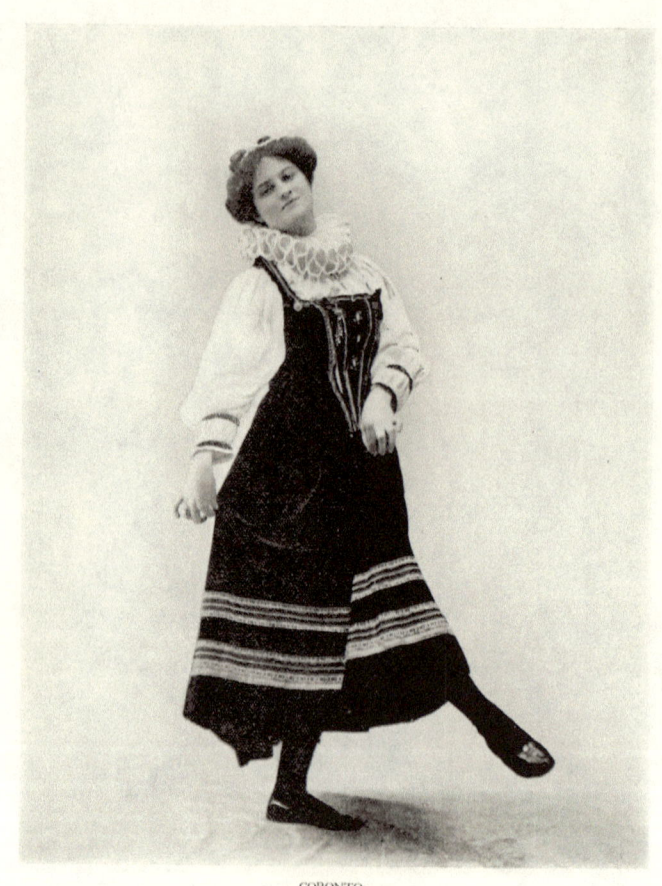

CORONTO.

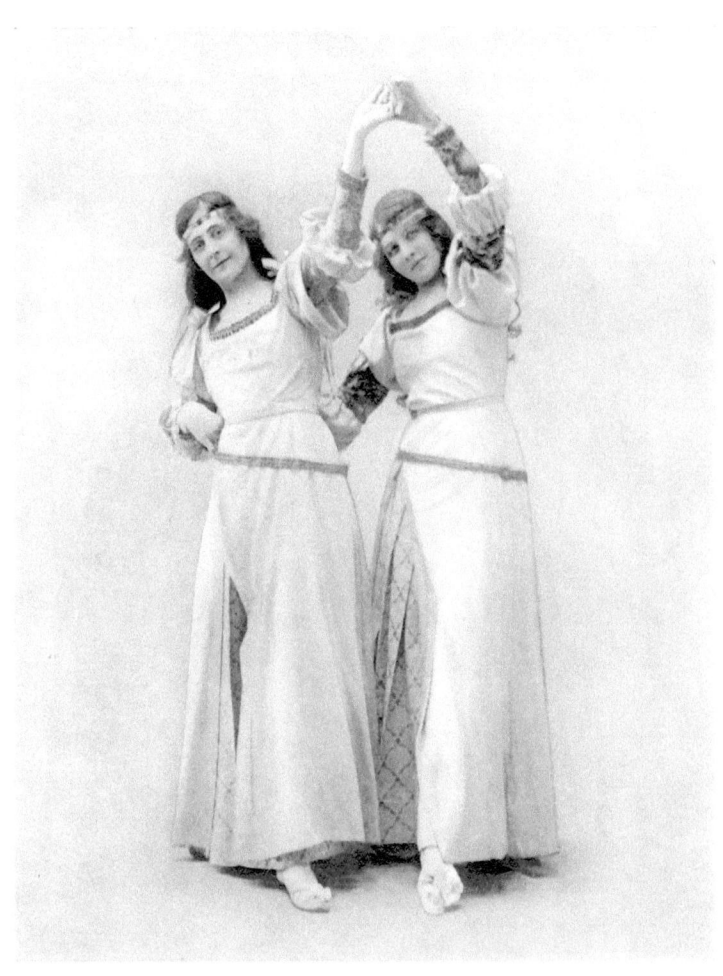

CHACONNE.

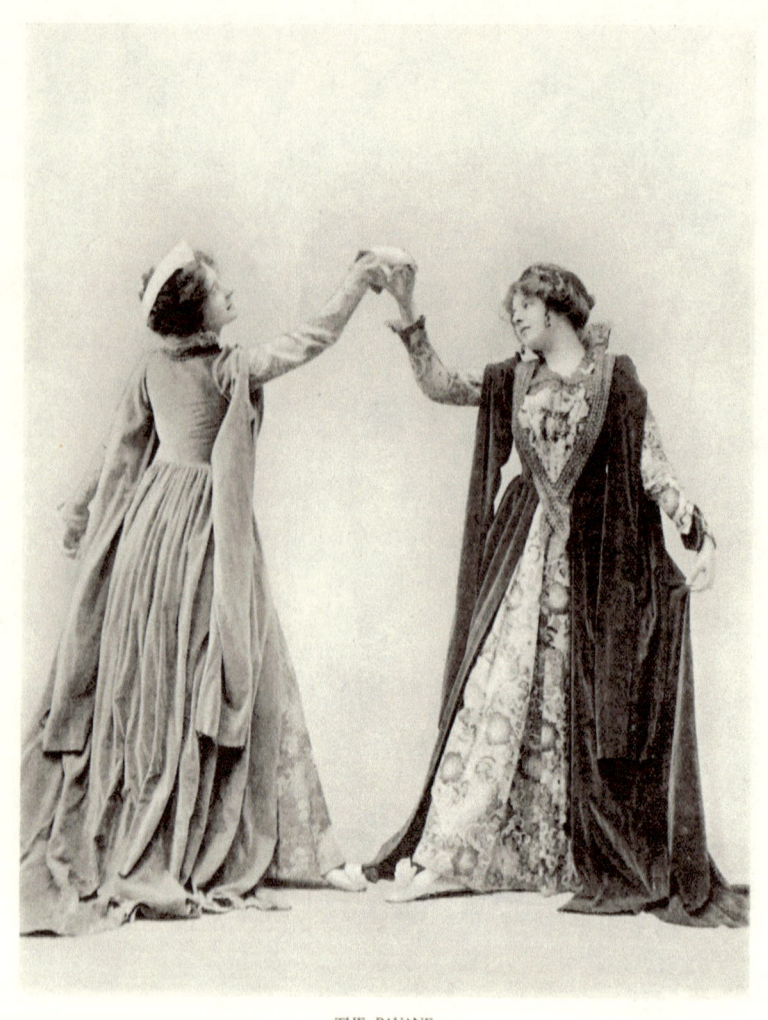

THE PAVANE.

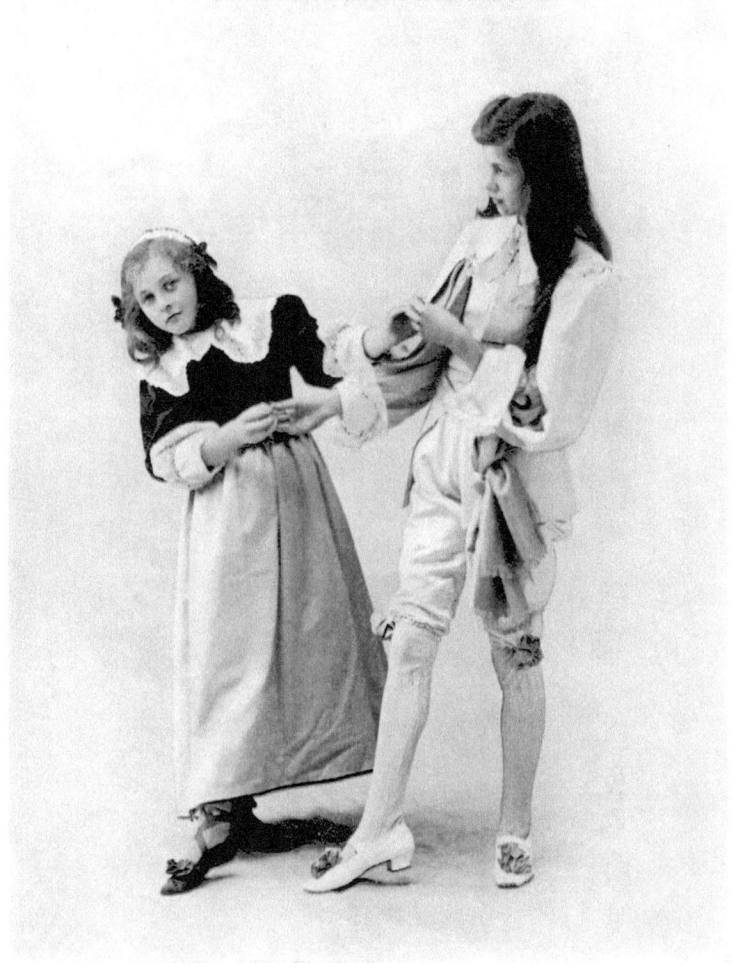

CANARIES.

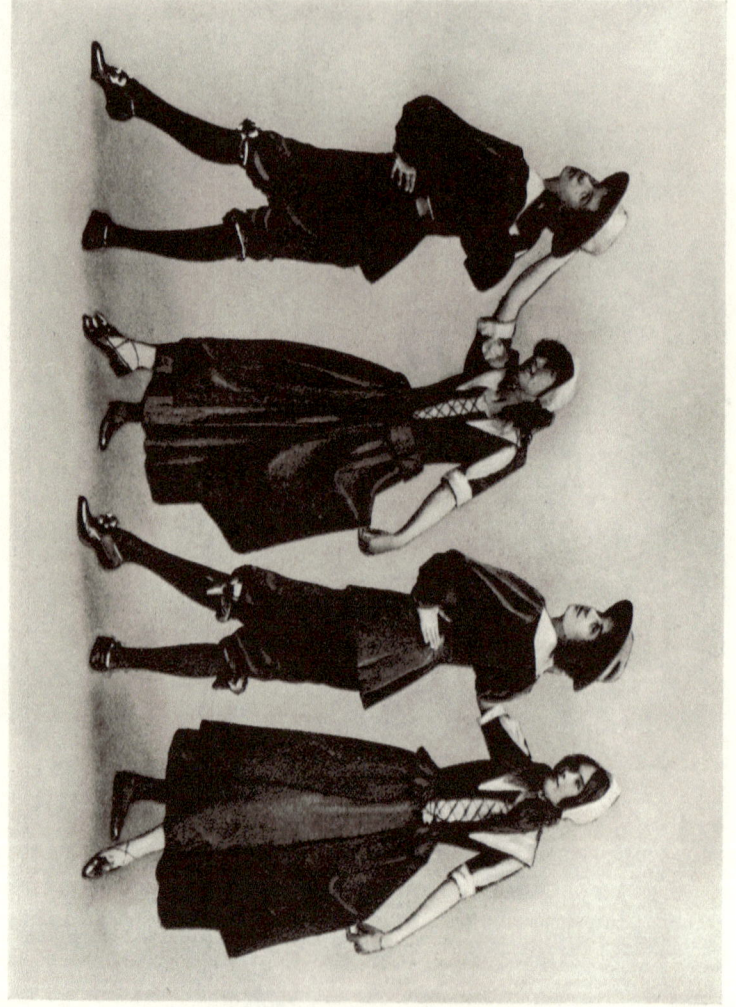

DARGASON.

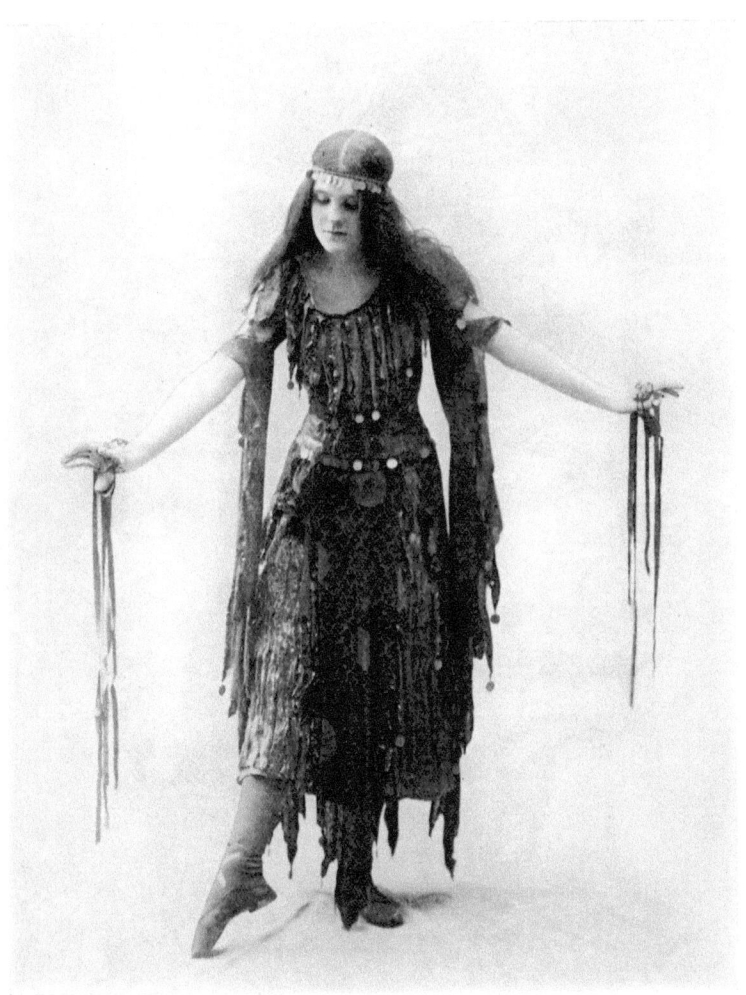

THE SARABANDE.

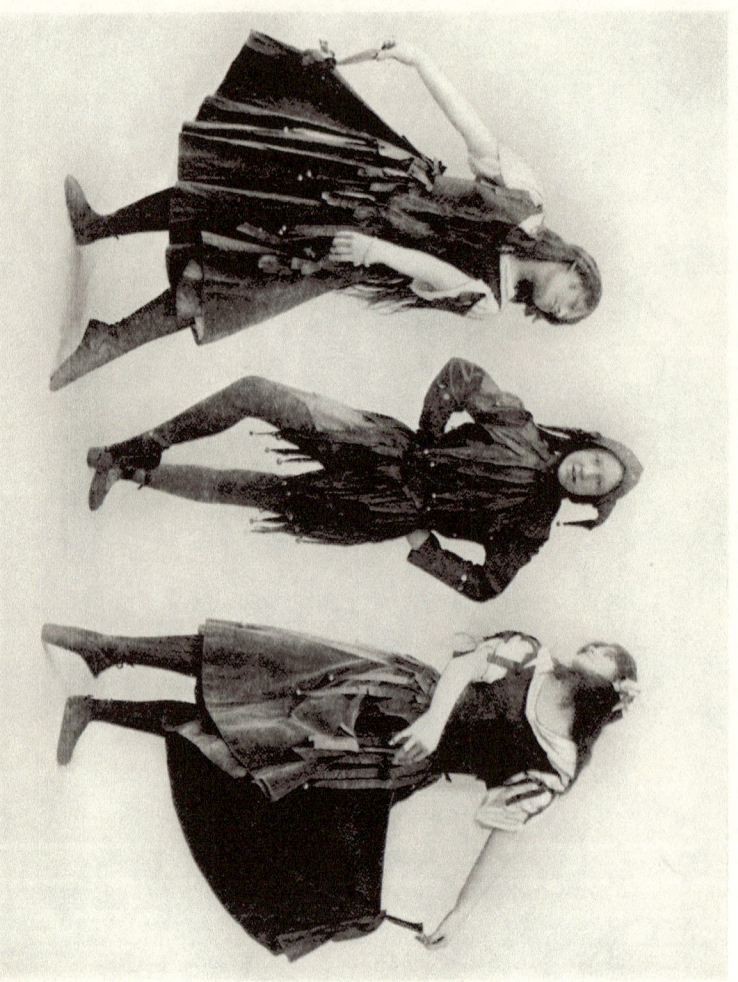

*The Illustrations of the Dances in this book
have been prepared under the direction of
Miss Nellie Chaplin, London.*

Dances of the Olden Time.

Royal Wedding.

COUNTRY DANCE.

First half of 18th century.

Allegro moderato.

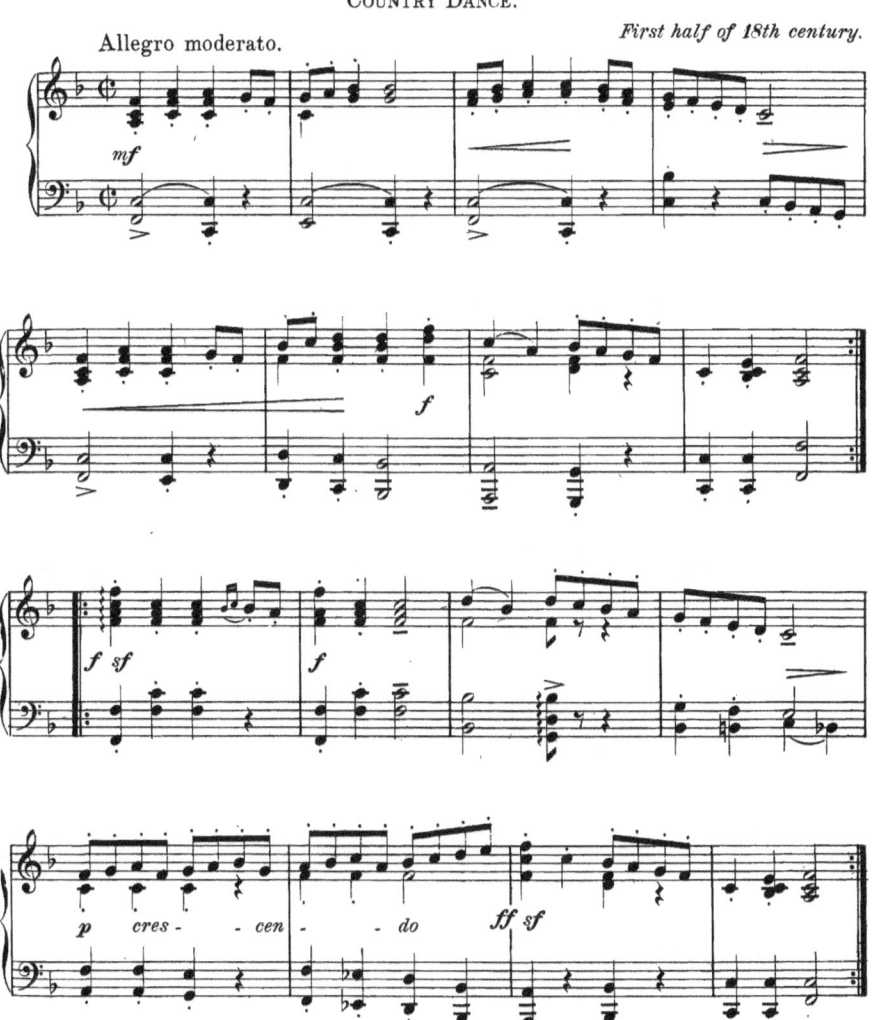

The Agreeable Society.

COTILLION.

C. 1780

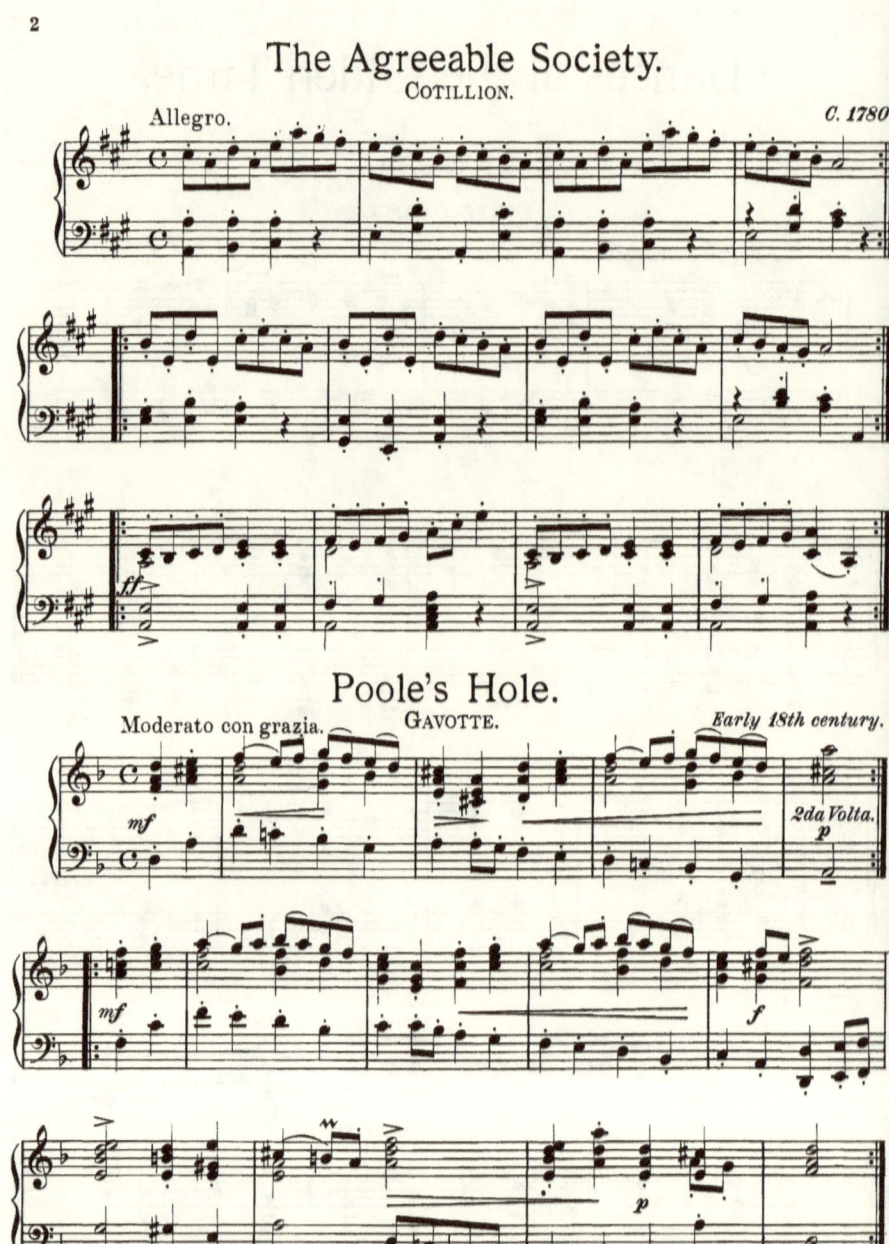

Poole's Hole.

GAVOTTE.

Early 18th century.

The Faithful Shepherd.

(The Rustic.)

ALLEMANDE SUISSE.

C. 1770.

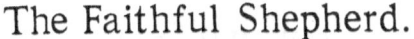

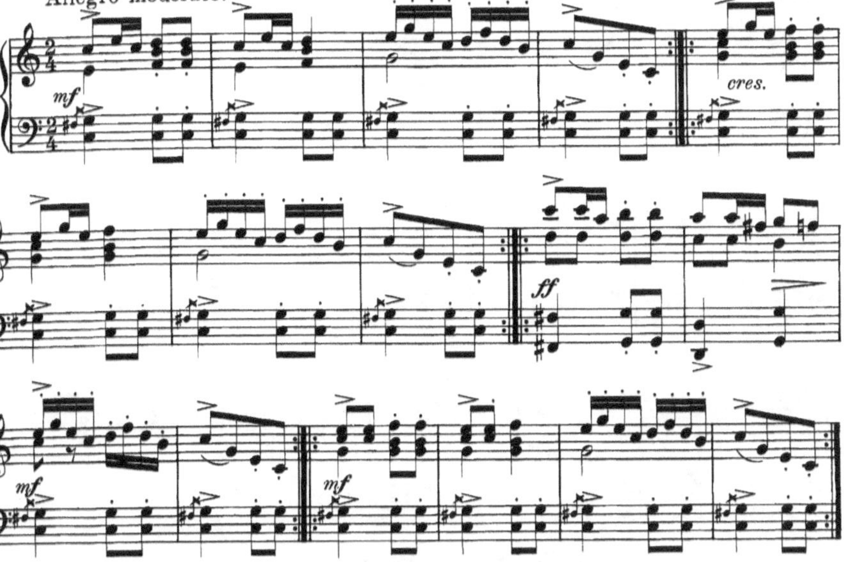

A la mode de France.

COURT DANCE.

17th century.

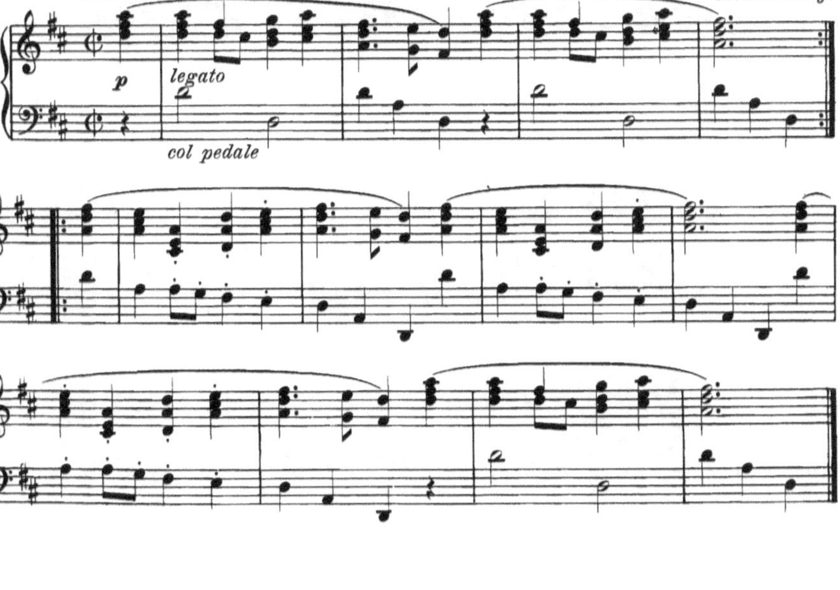

Fox and Geese.
COUNTRY DANCE.

Vivamente.

Middle of 18th century.

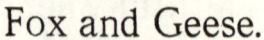

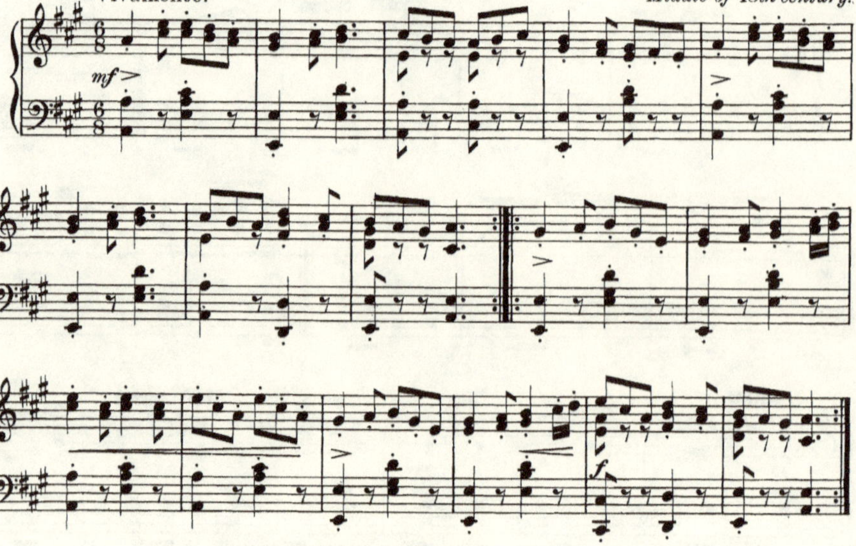

Mad Robin.
COUNTRY DANCE.

Allegro moderato.

1700.

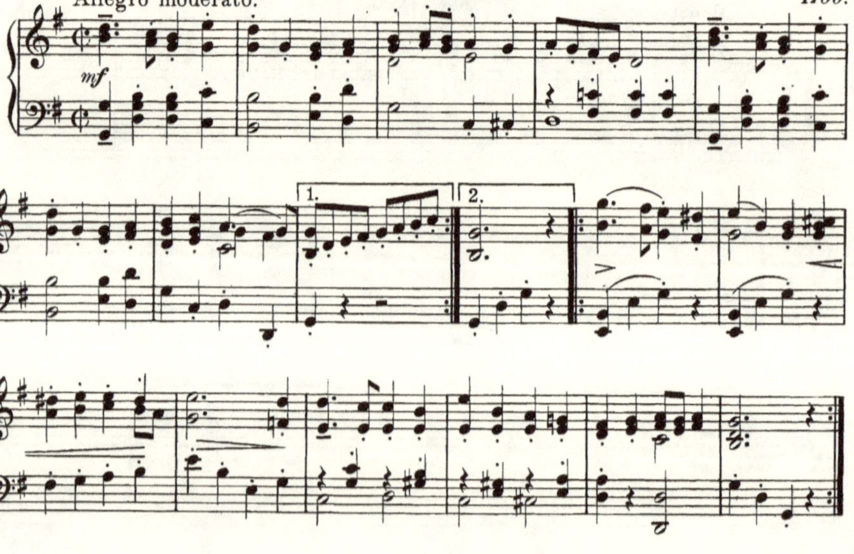

E-O.

COUNTRY DANCE.

First half of 18th century.

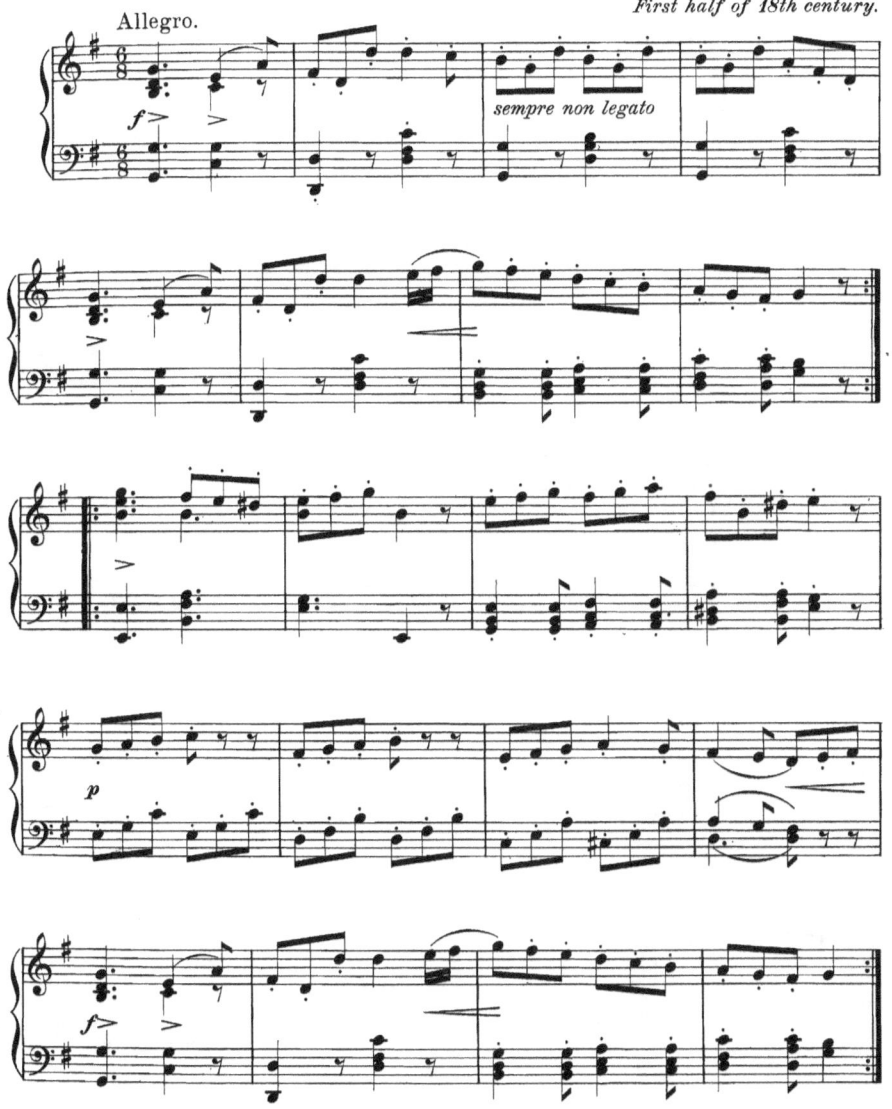

6

Bourree.

A tempo giusto.

Early 18th century.

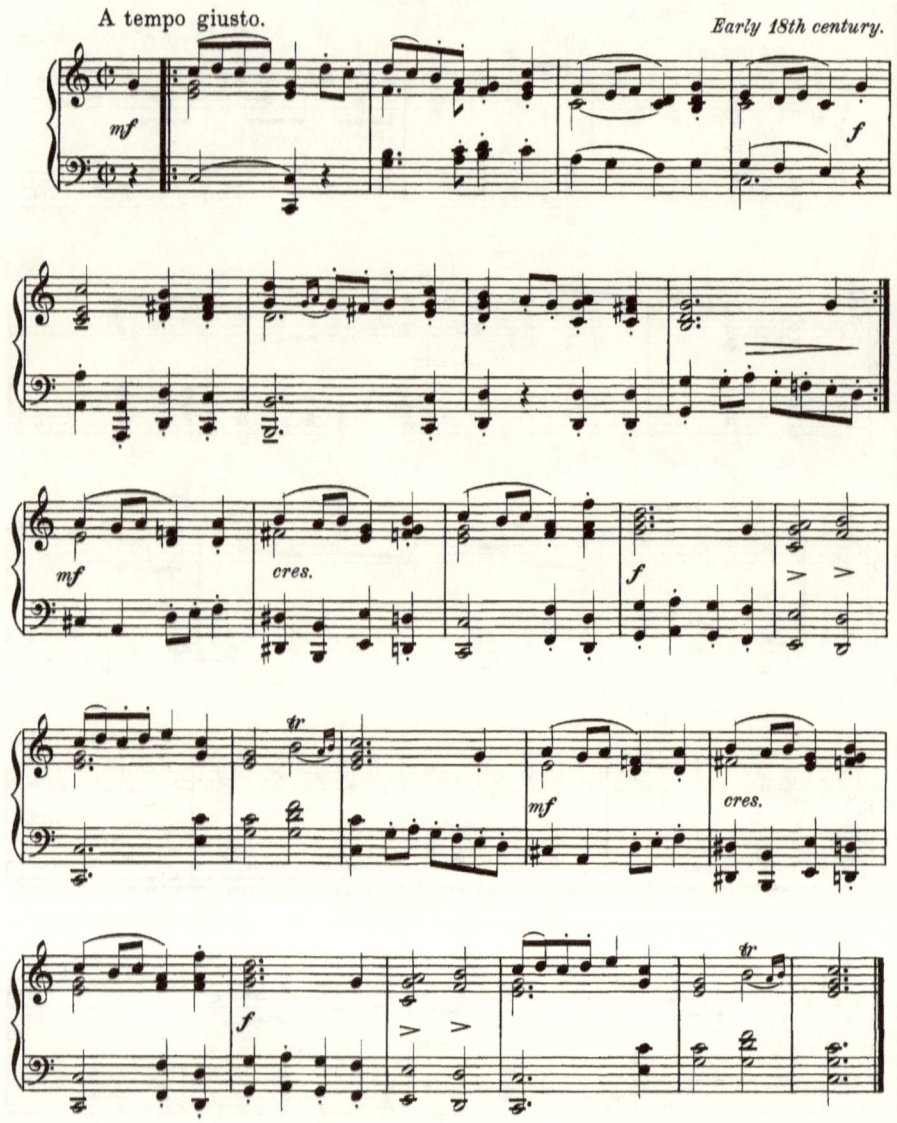

Hampstead Heath.

COUNTRY DANCE.

Moderato con grazia.

1719.

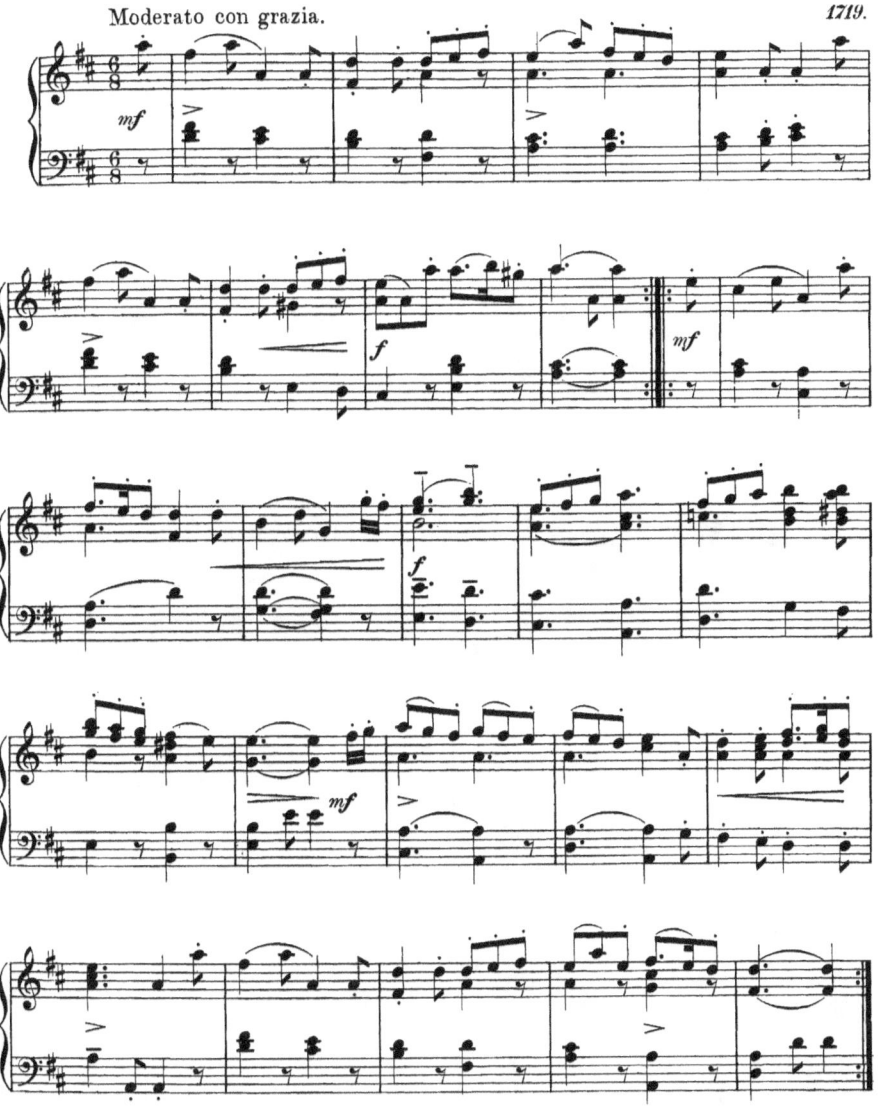

The 11th of September.

MINUET.

Con grazia.

C. 1760.

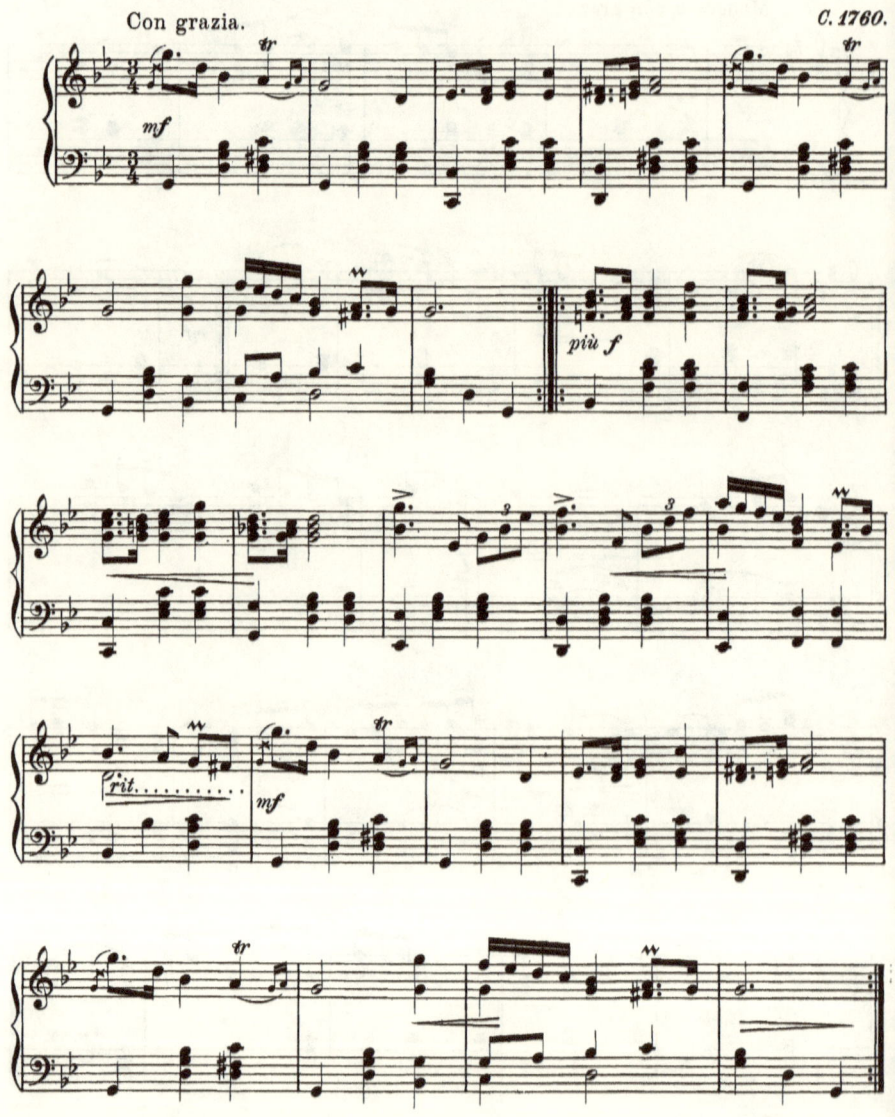

Maid's Morris.

17th century.

Ash Wednesday.

Jig.

C. 1750.

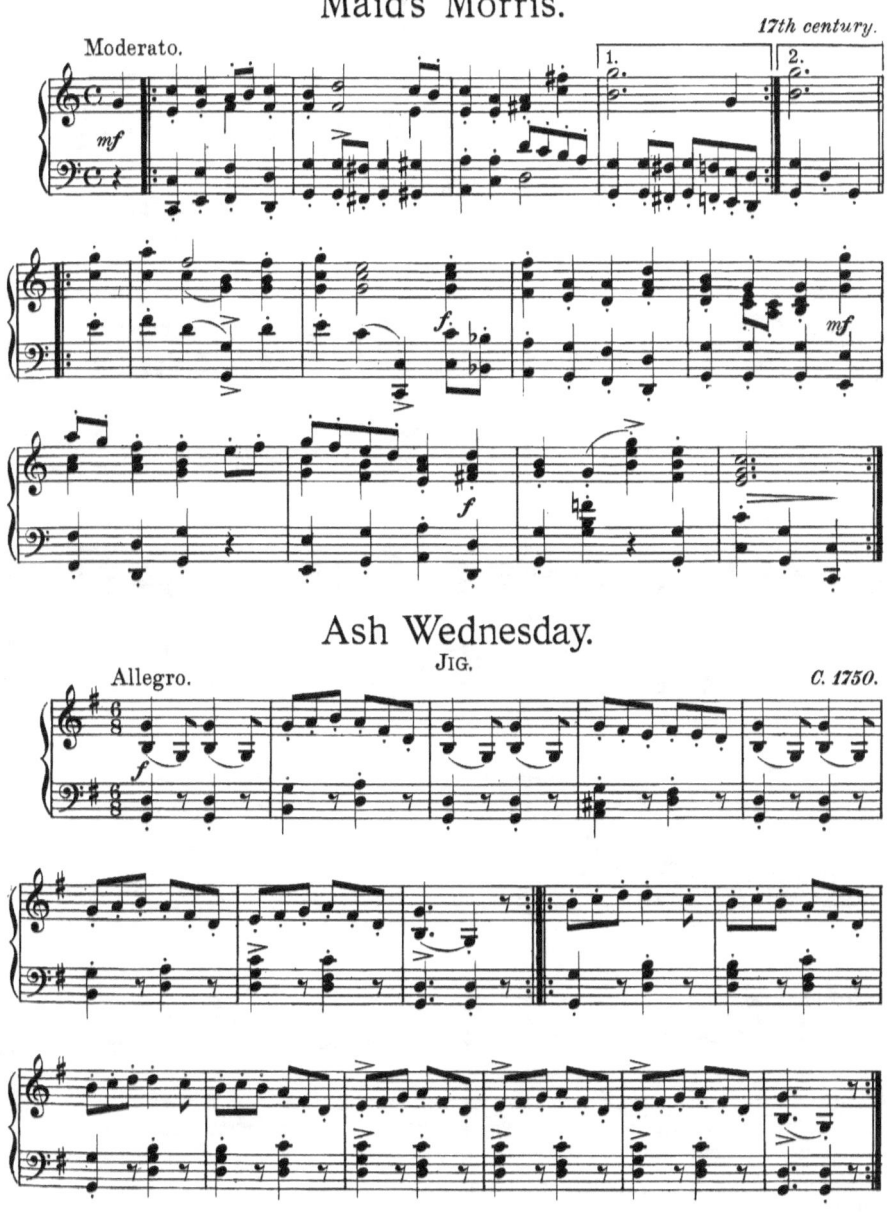

Stanes' Morris.[*]

1650.

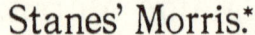

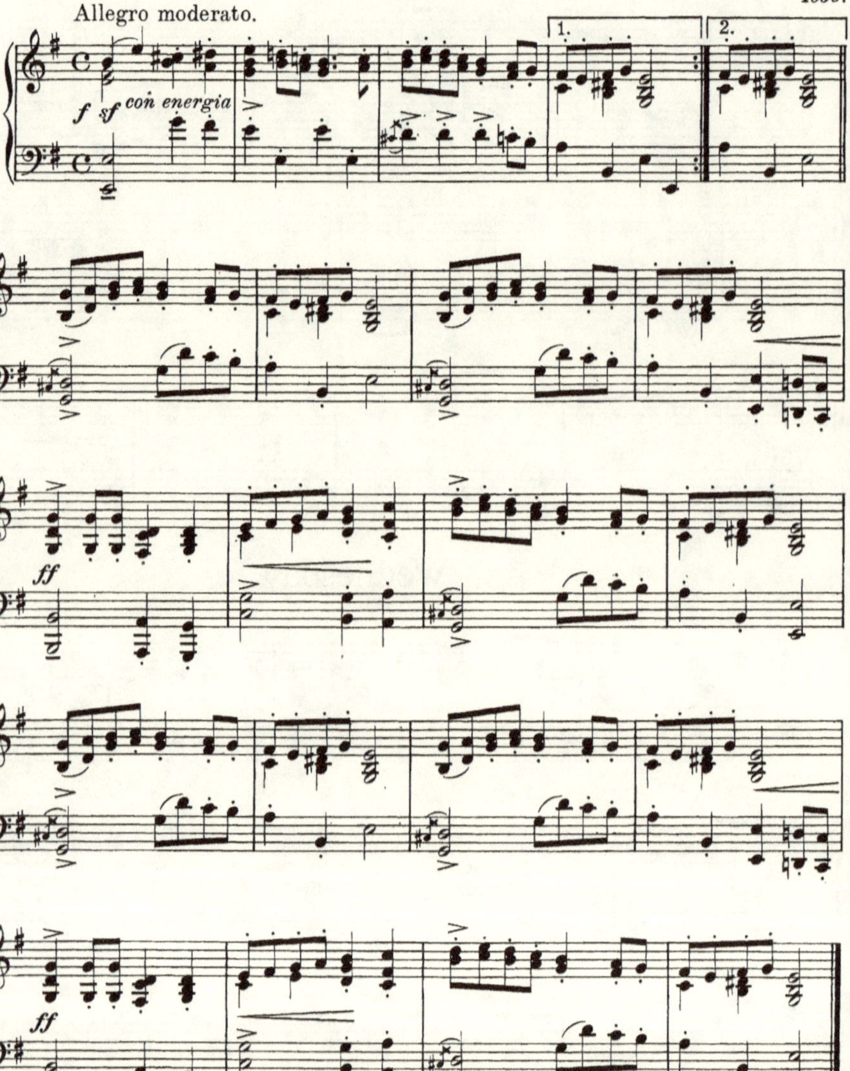

* Wright's Collection of *Pleasant and Merry Humours* C. 1720, contains a tune entitled "Stanes Morris" which is quite different from the above.

Saraband.*

Lento con molto espressione.

17th century.

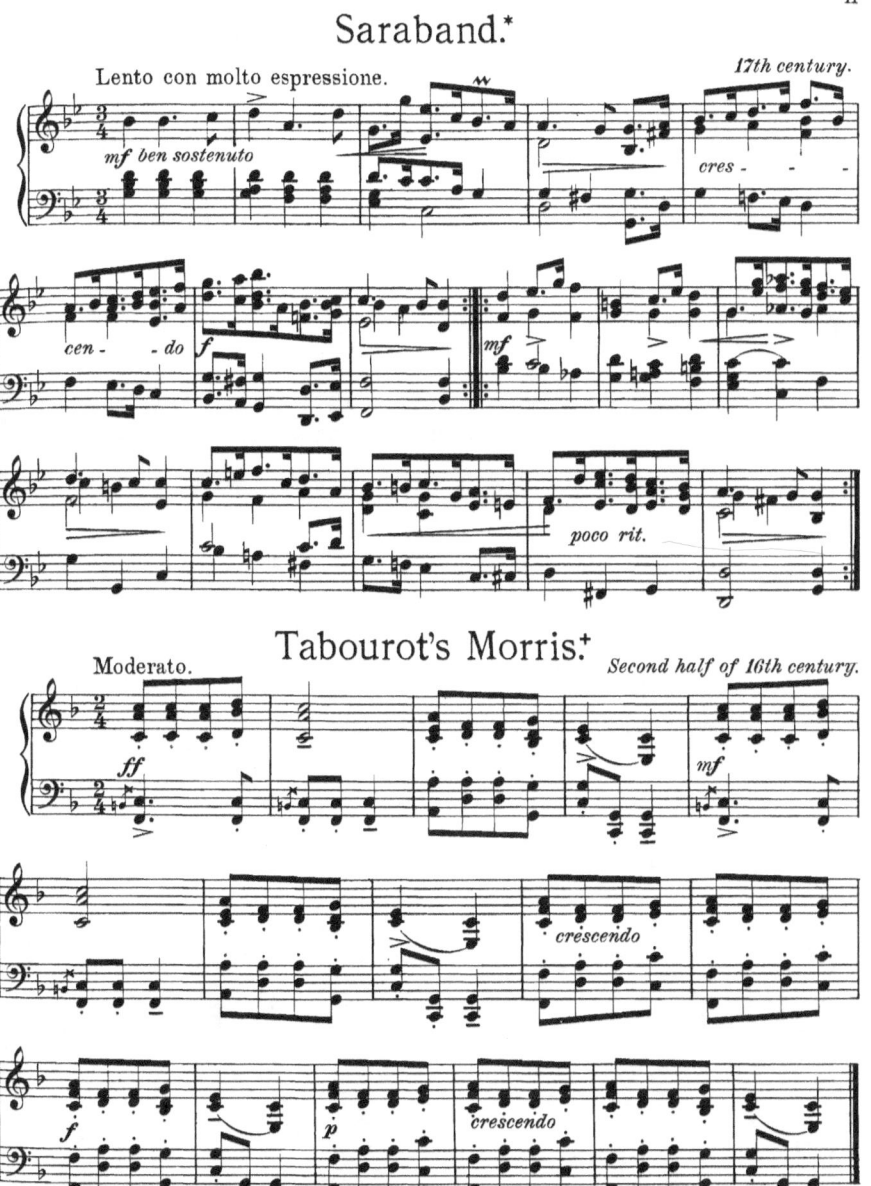

Tabourot's Morris.†

Moderato.

Second half of 16th century.

---

* The composition of England's greatest musician Henry Purcell, who was born 1658 and died 1695.

† From Jehan Tabourot's *Orchésographie* printed at Langres in 1589.

Kettle Drum.

COUNTRY DANCE.

2nd half of 17th century.

Allegro moderato.

Brisk and Airy.

TRIPLE MEASURE HORNPIPE.

Early 18th century.

Allegro.

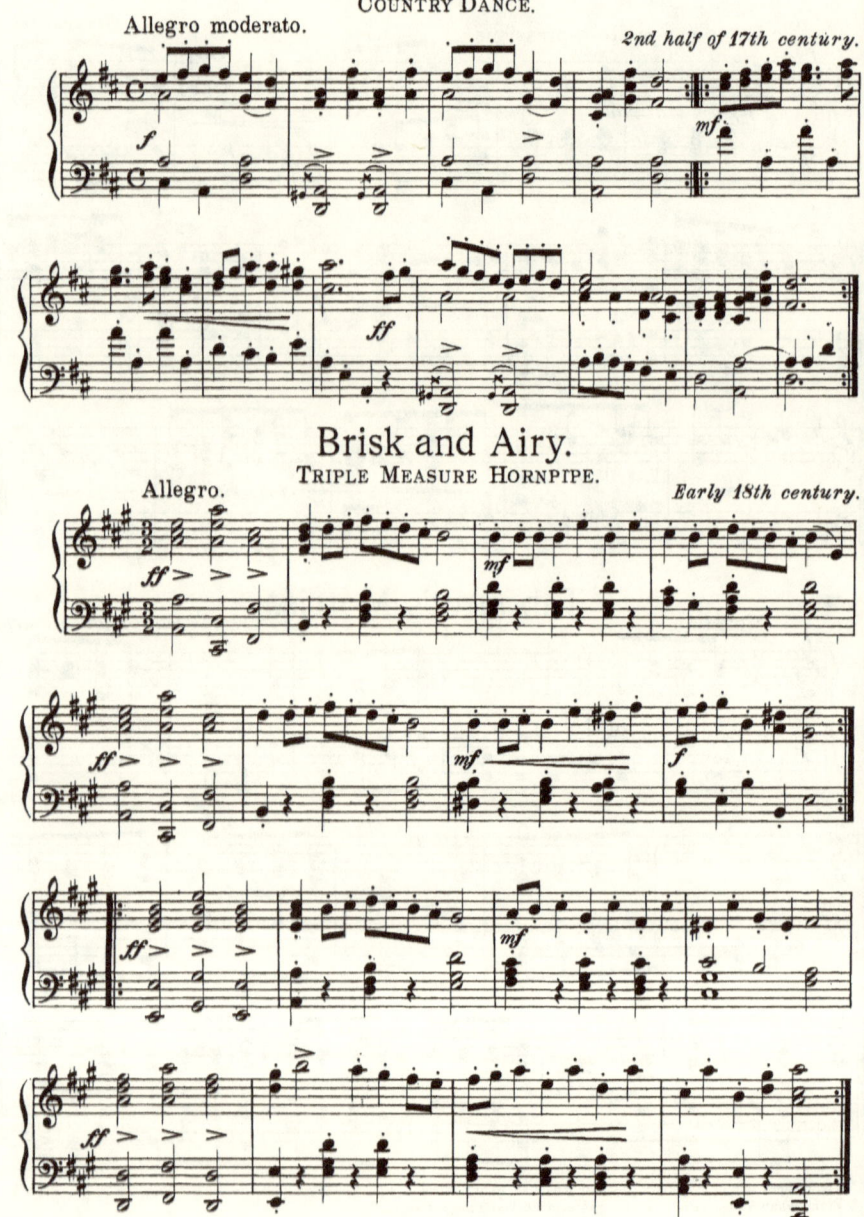

Can'st Thou not weave Bonelace.

JIG.

C. 1730.

The Gimcrack.

COTILLION.

First half of 18th century.

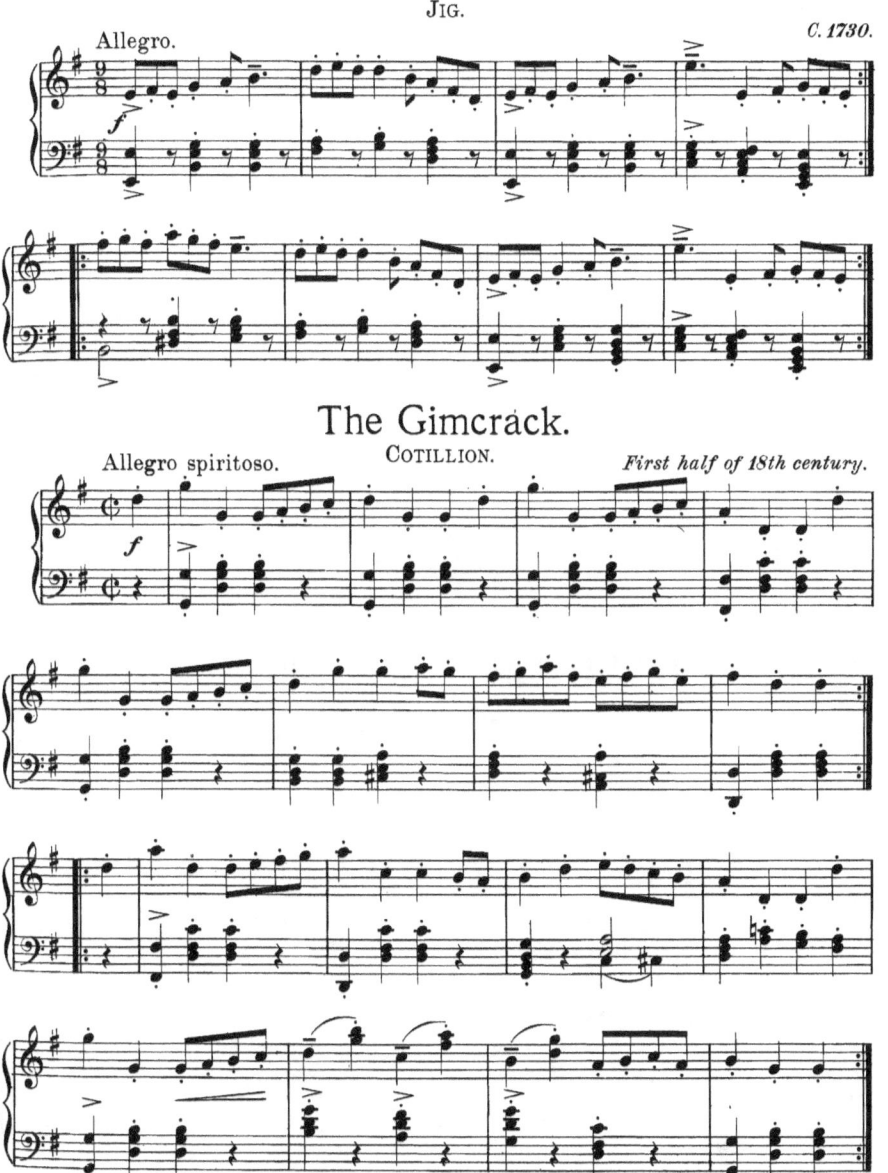

Gavotte.

C. 1765.

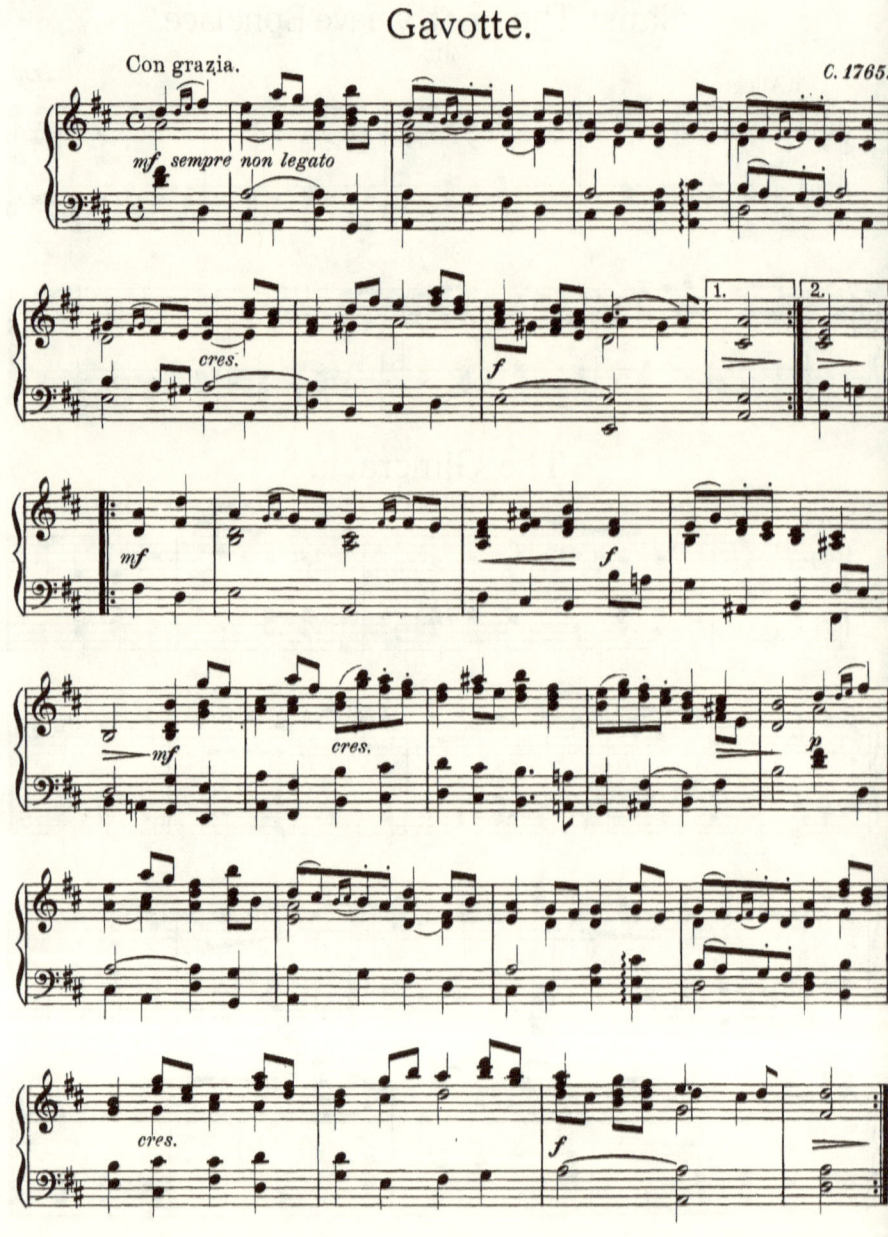

Peace and Plenty.

COTILLION.

C. 1770.

Allegretto.

mf non legato

Marionettes.

COTILLION.

C. 1770.

Vivace.

mf non legato

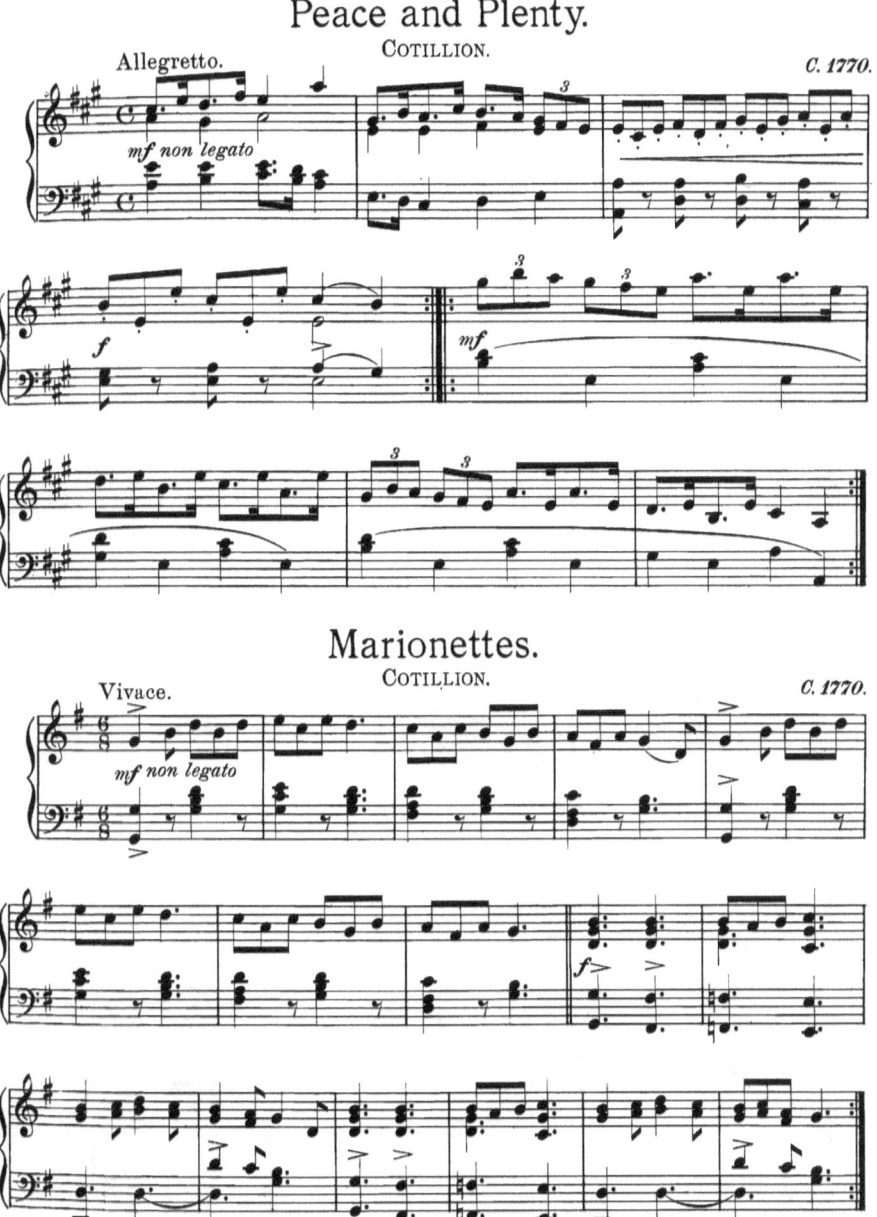

Enfield Common.

Triple Measure Hornpipe.

Con spirito.

mf

1716

Brighton Camp, or, The Girl I left behind me.

Morris Dance.

Vivamente.

mf

C. 1810

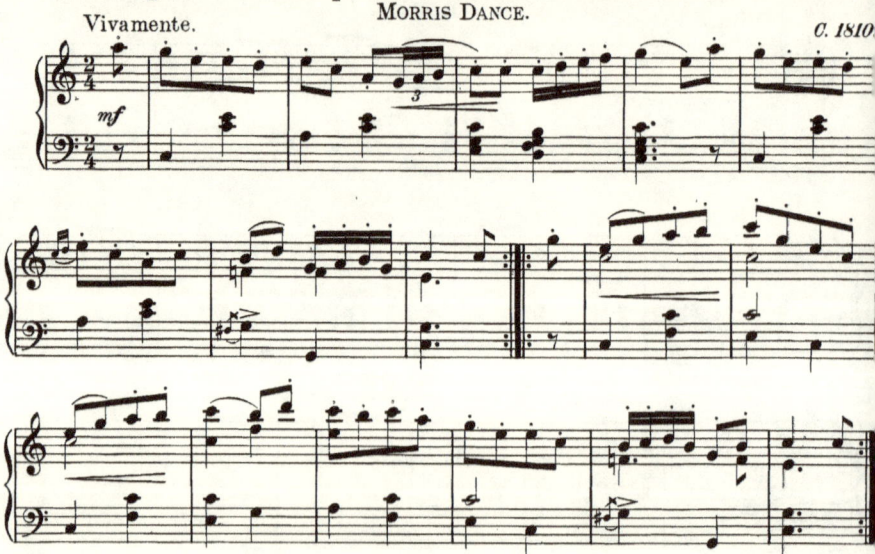

The Barley Mow.

COUNTRY DANCE.

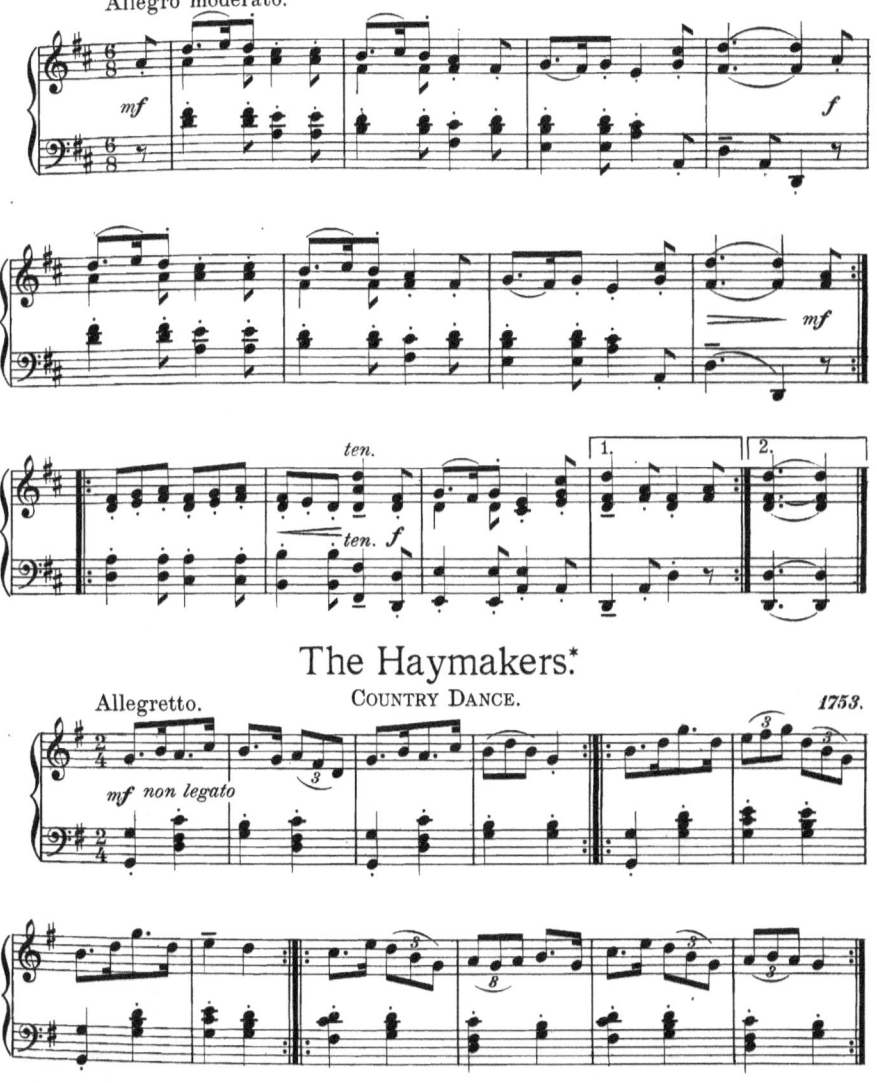

The Haymakers.*

COUNTRY DANCE.

1753.

* Mr. Frank Kidson informs me that this well-known Country Dance, which has retained its popularity to the present day, occurs in a Pantomime called *Fortunatus* written in 1753 by James Oswald, a Scottish musician, who settled in London in 1741 and became "Chamber Composer to His Majesty George III."

Three Sheep Skins.*
MORRIS DANCE.

1782.

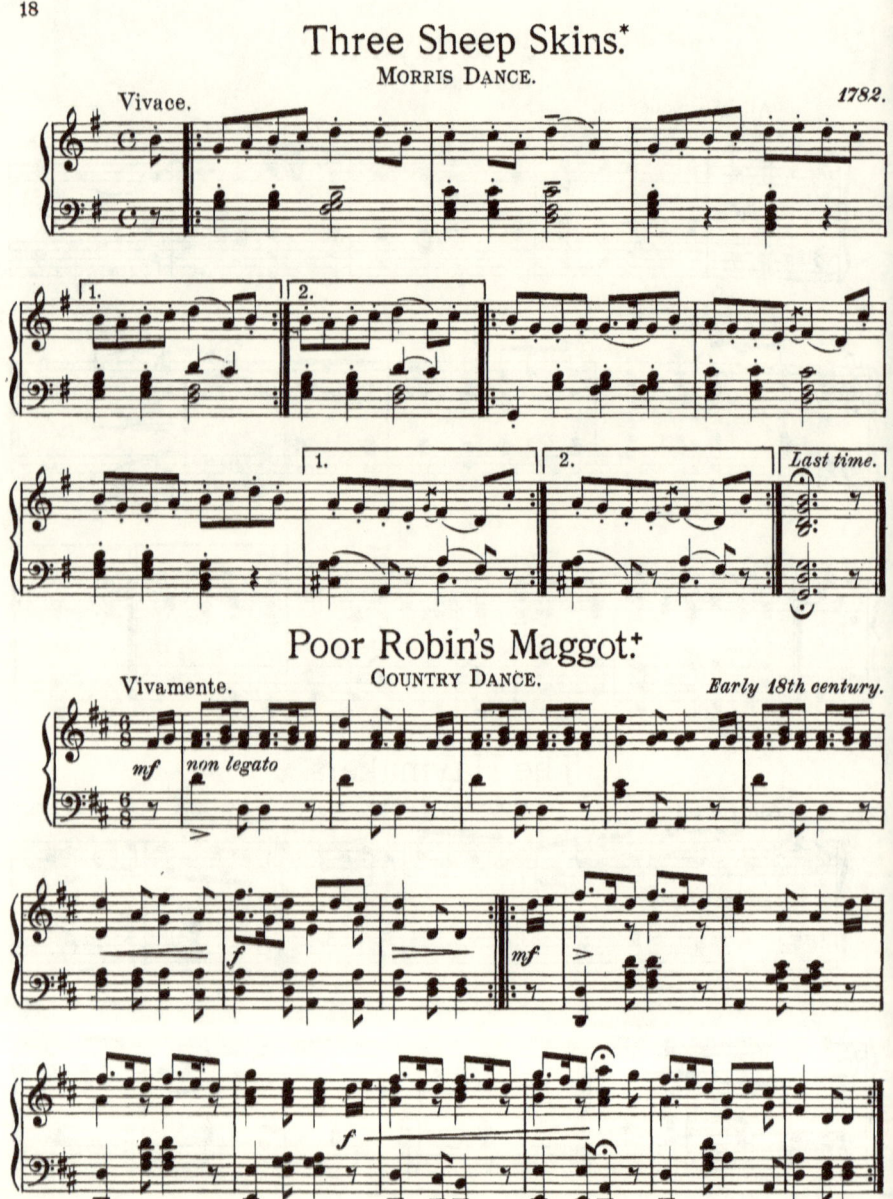

Poor Robin's Maggot.†
COUNTRY DANCE.

Early 18th century.

* An early version of this old tune was printed in Playford's *Dancing-Master.*
† Maggot means fancy or whim.

Ten Pound Lass.

COUNTRY DANCE.

Early 18th century.

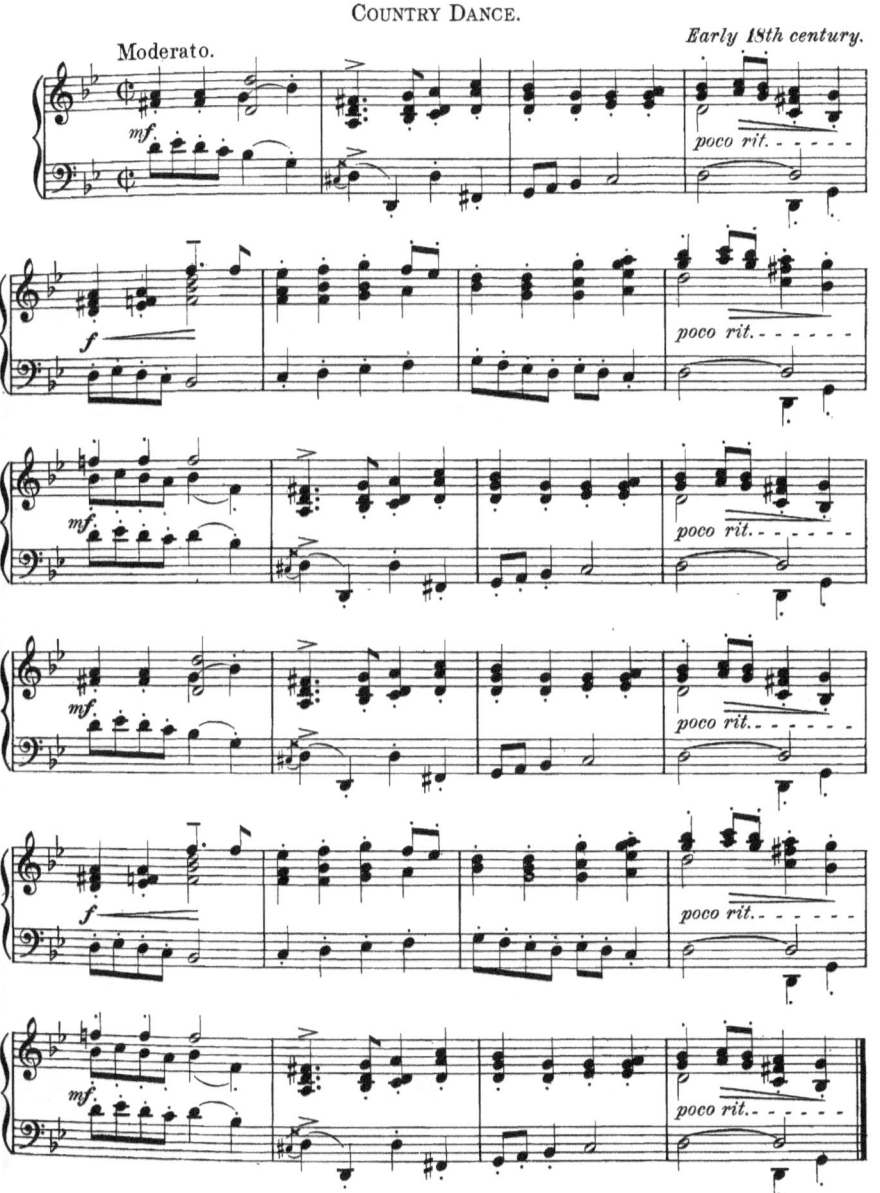

The Old Rigadoon.

Early 18th century.

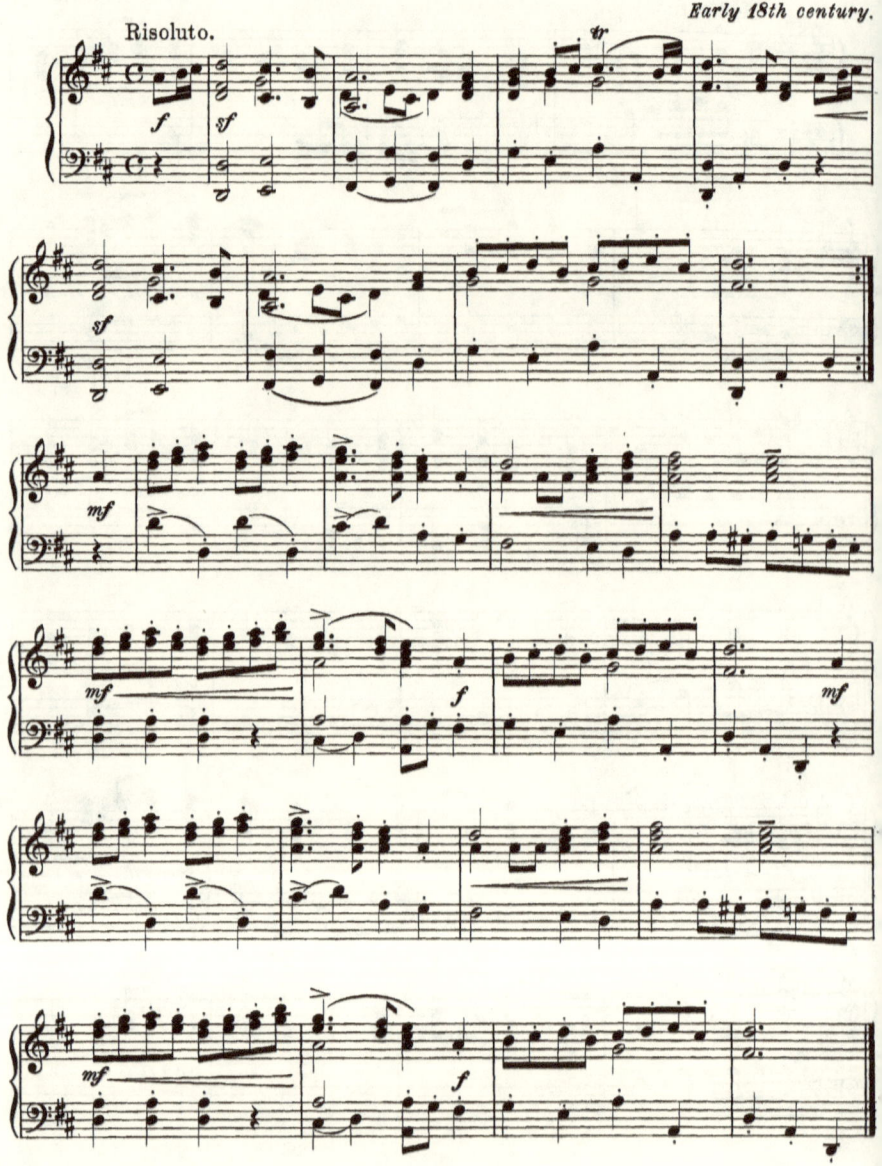

All in a Garden green.

Country Dance.

16th century.

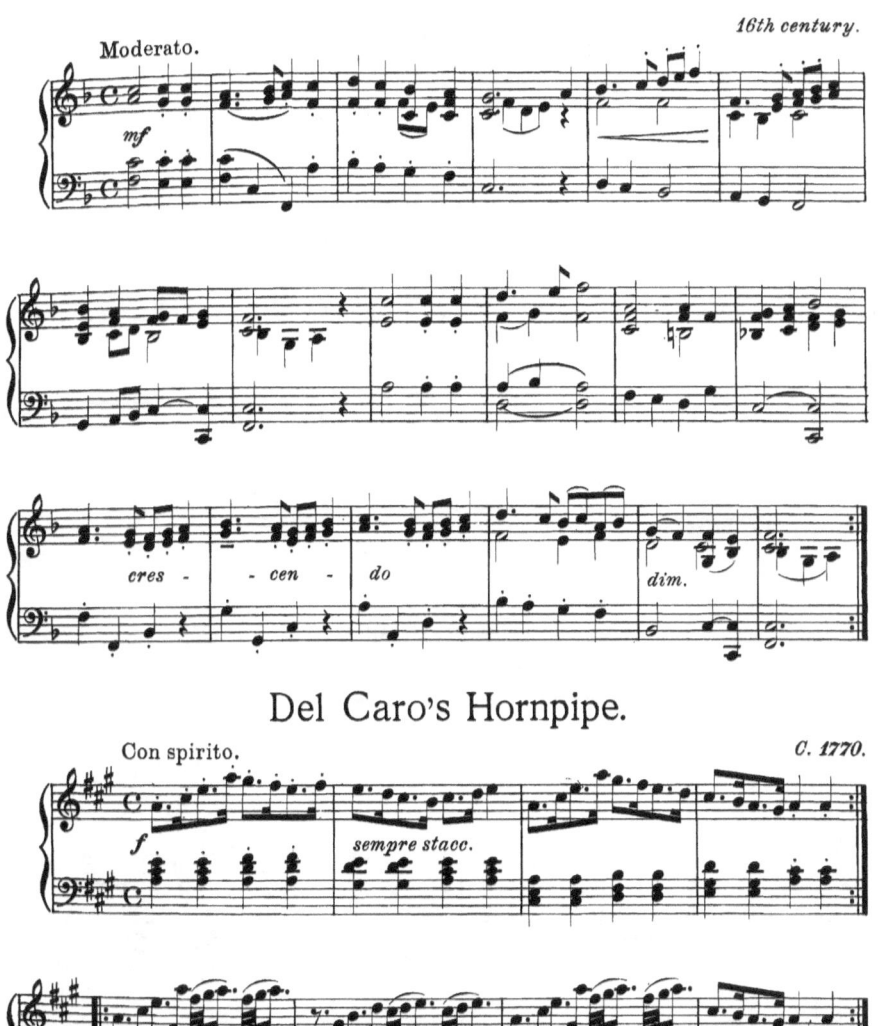

Del Caro's Hornpipe.

A Morris Dance.

C. 1720.

Allegro moderato.

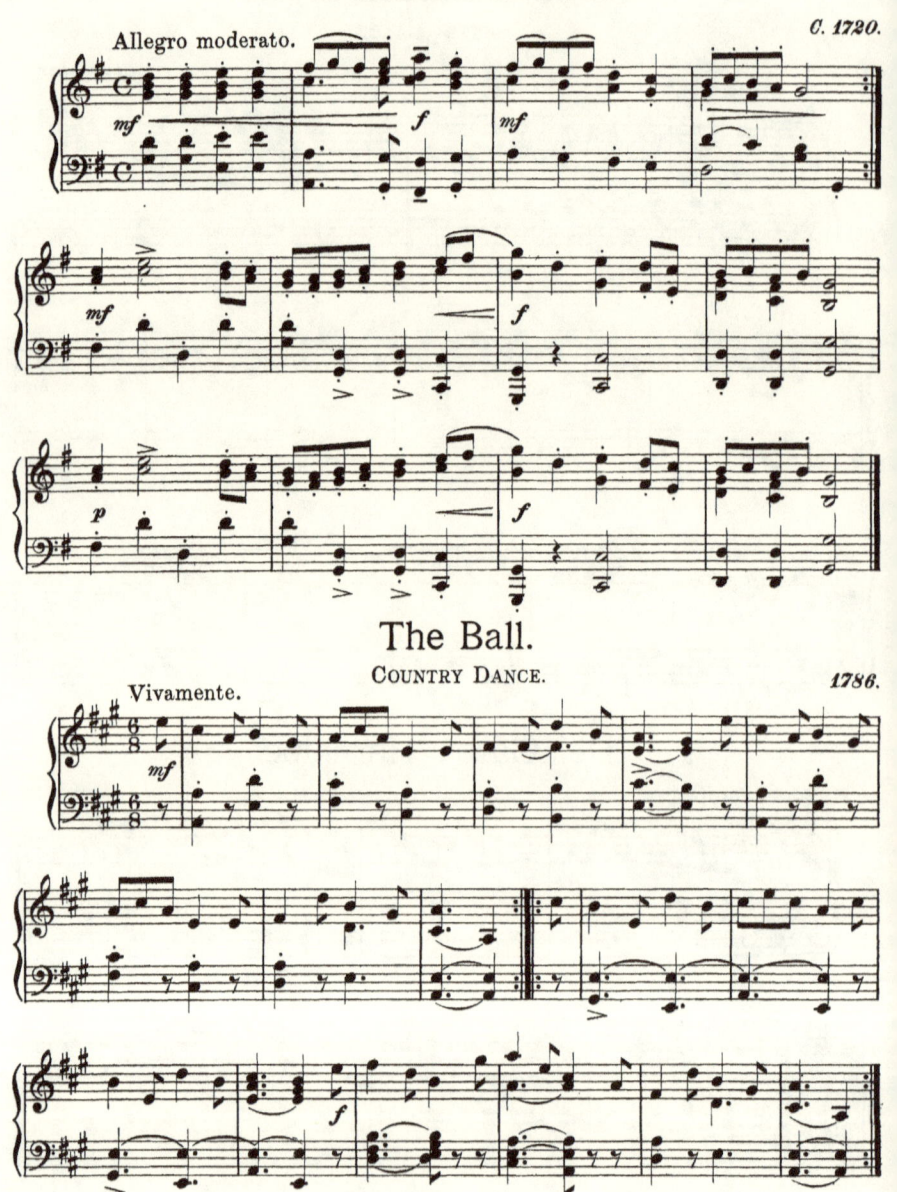

The Ball.

COUNTRY DANCE.

1786.

Vivamente.

Lady Smith's Minuet.

Con grazia.

18th century.

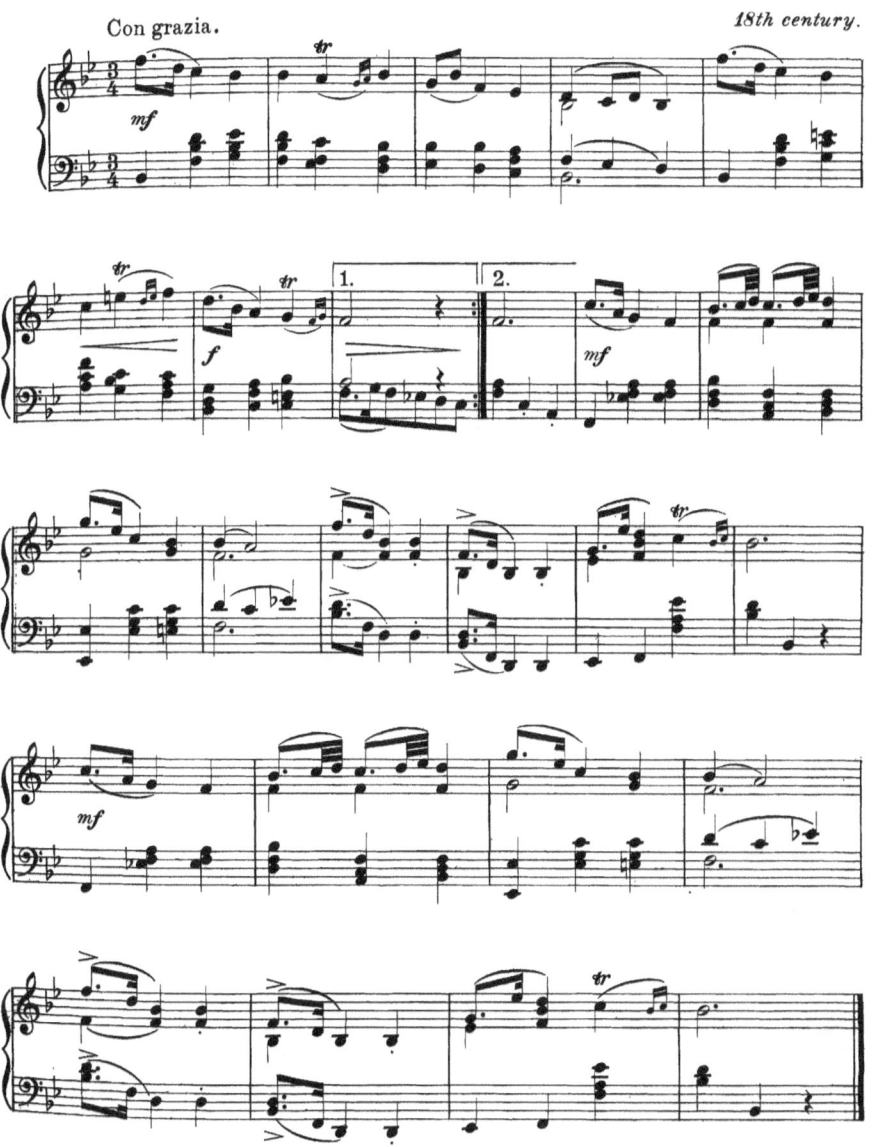

Sweet William.

BOURREE.

Late 17th century.

A tempo giusto.

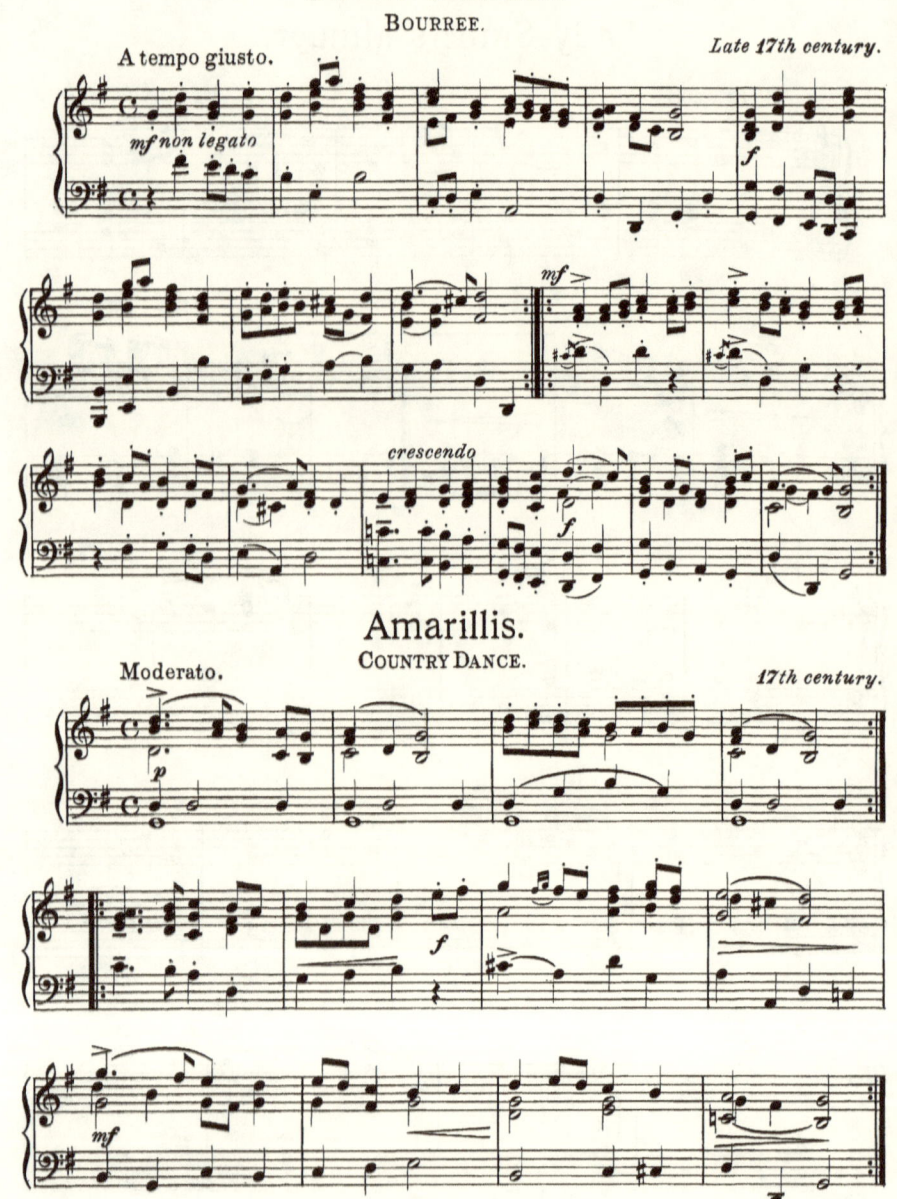

Amarillis.

COUNTRY DANCE.

17th century.

Moderato.

On a Bank of Flowers.*
COUNTRY DANCE.

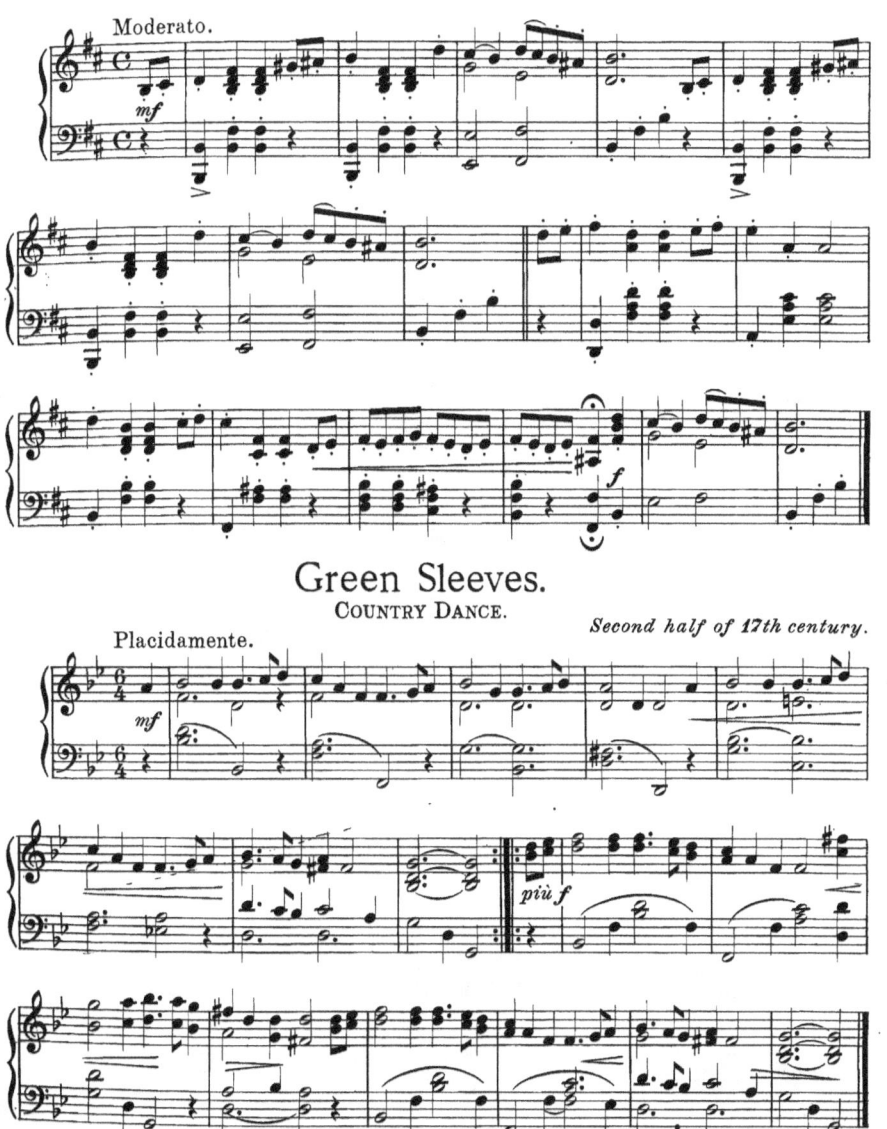

Green Sleeves.
COUNTRY DANCE.

Second half of 17th century.

* Said to be the composition of J. E. Galliard, a clever German musician who resided in England from 1706 until his death in 1749.

Goddesses.*

COUNTRY DANCE.

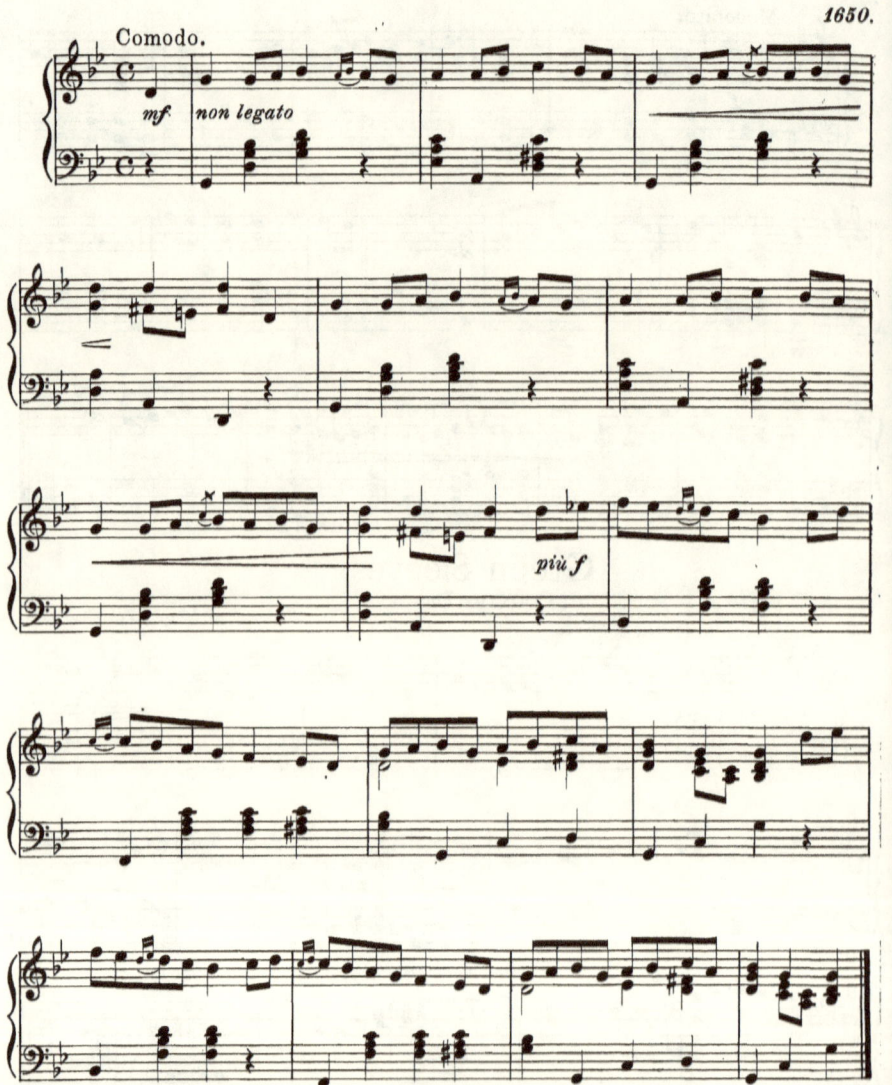

*A less florid version of this tune is preserved in the Fitzwilliam Virginal Book as "Quodling's Delight."

Buttered Pease.*

MORRIS DANCE.

C. 1748.

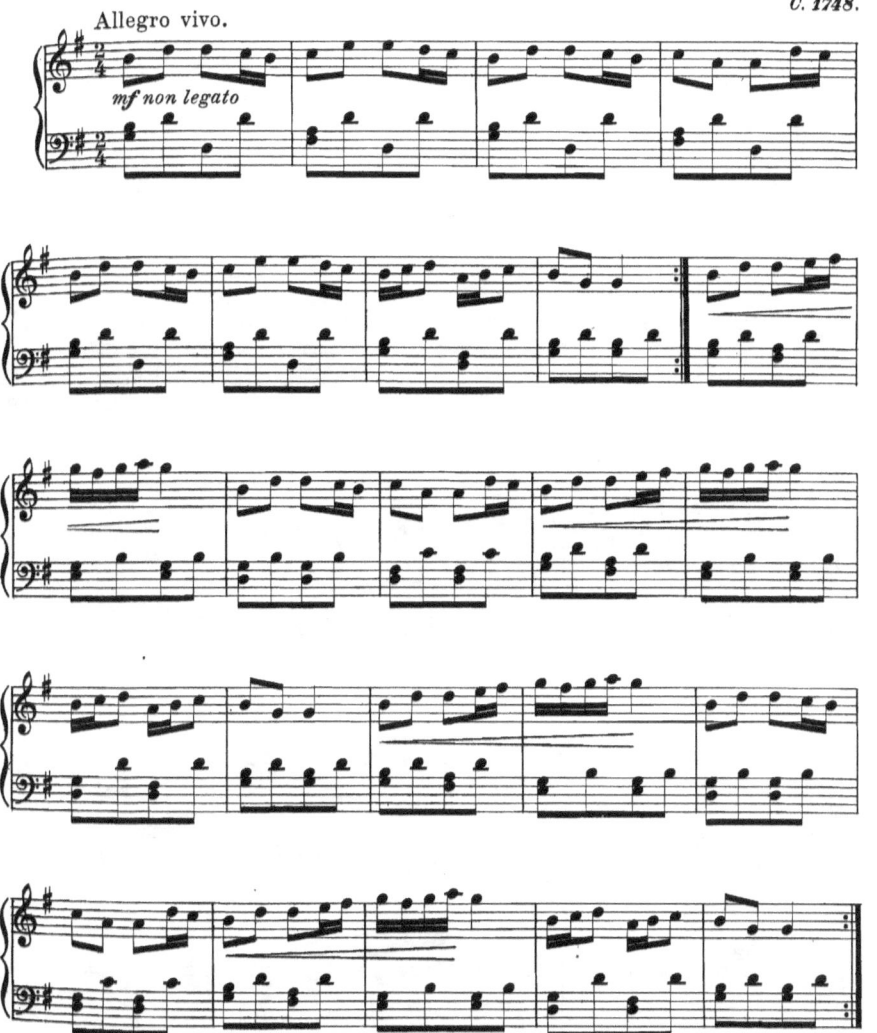

Kemp's Jigg.

Allegro moderato.

17th century

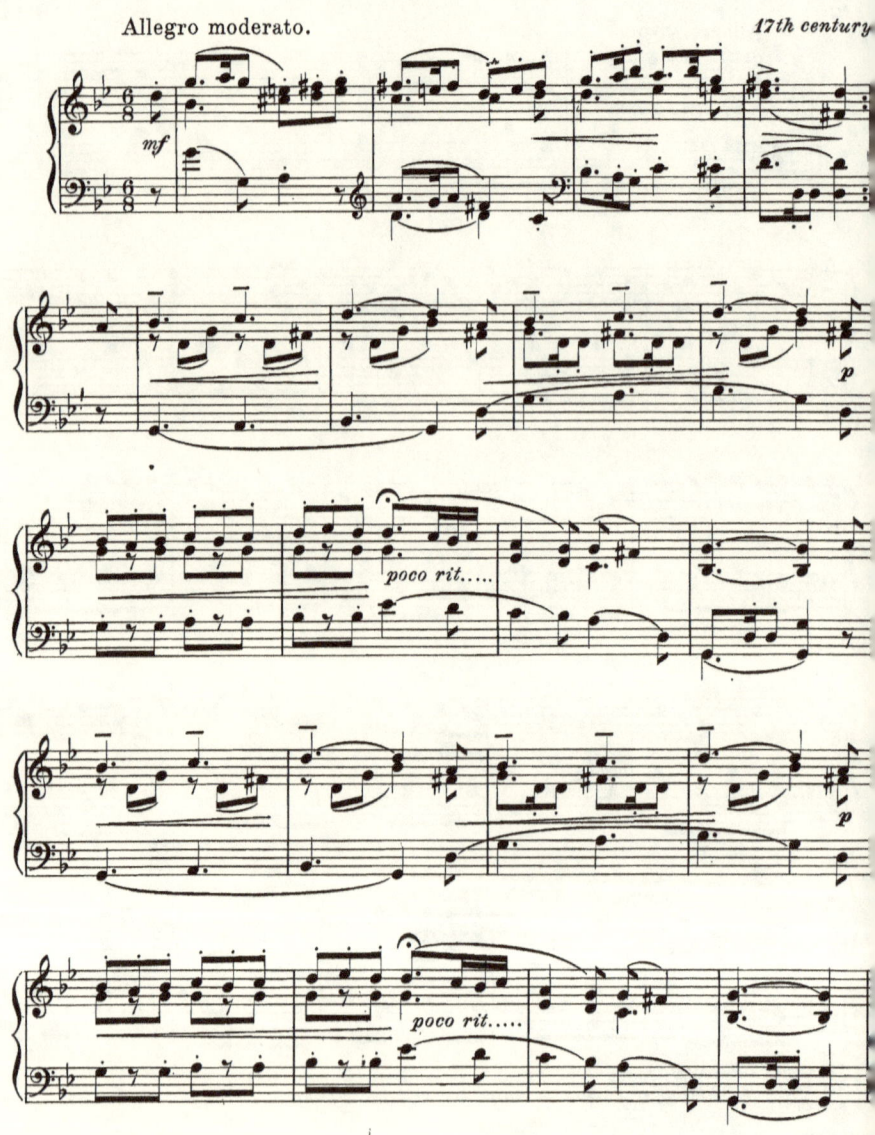

Round O.*

MINUET.

Con grazia.

C. 1700.

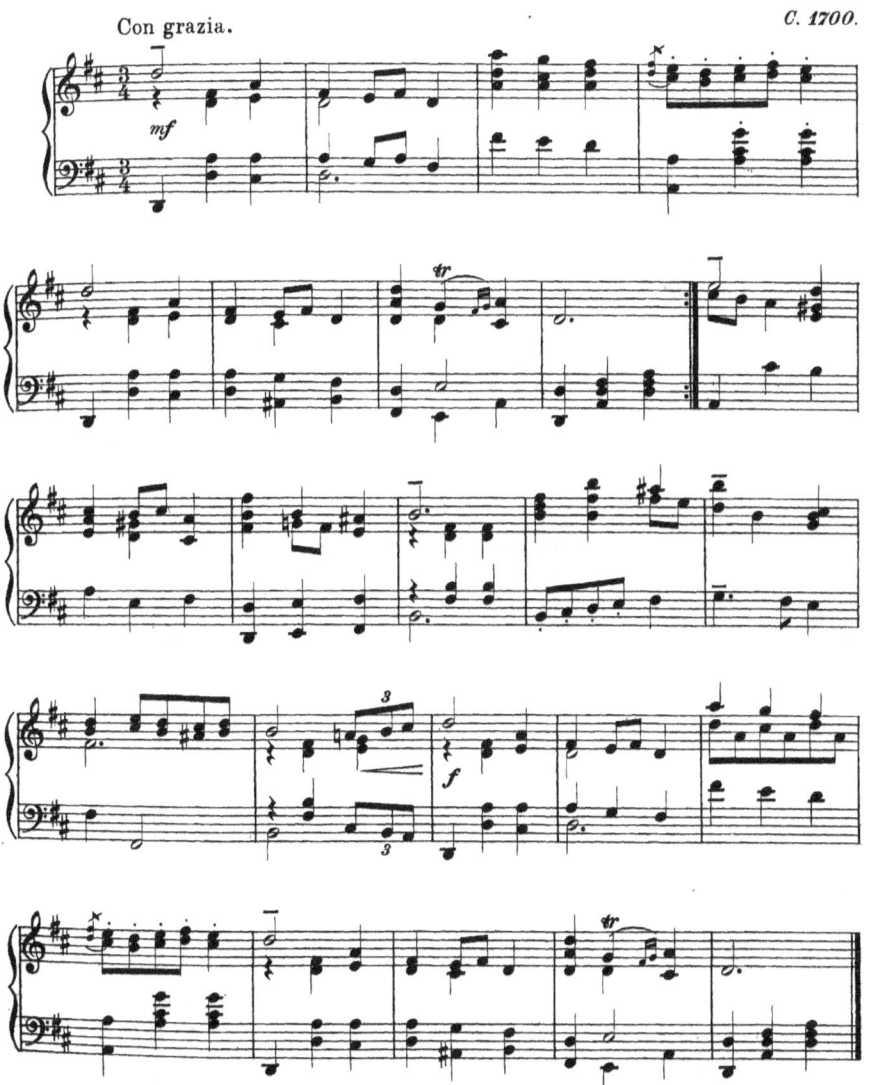

* From a manuscript book of dance tunes written about 1700.

Trenchmore.
COUNTRY DANCE.

17th century.

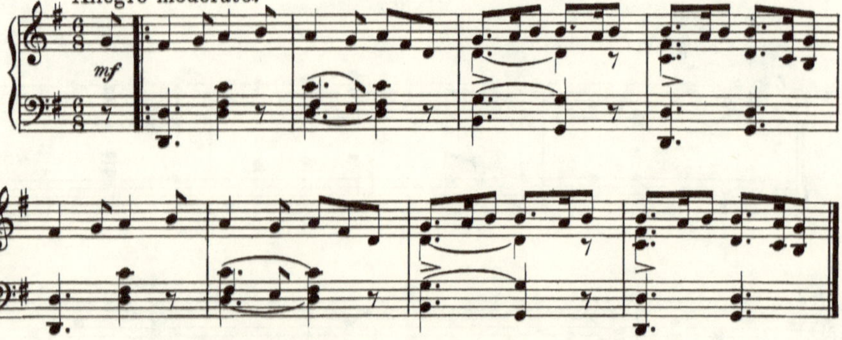

Once I loved a Maiden fair.
COUNTRY DANCE.

1650.

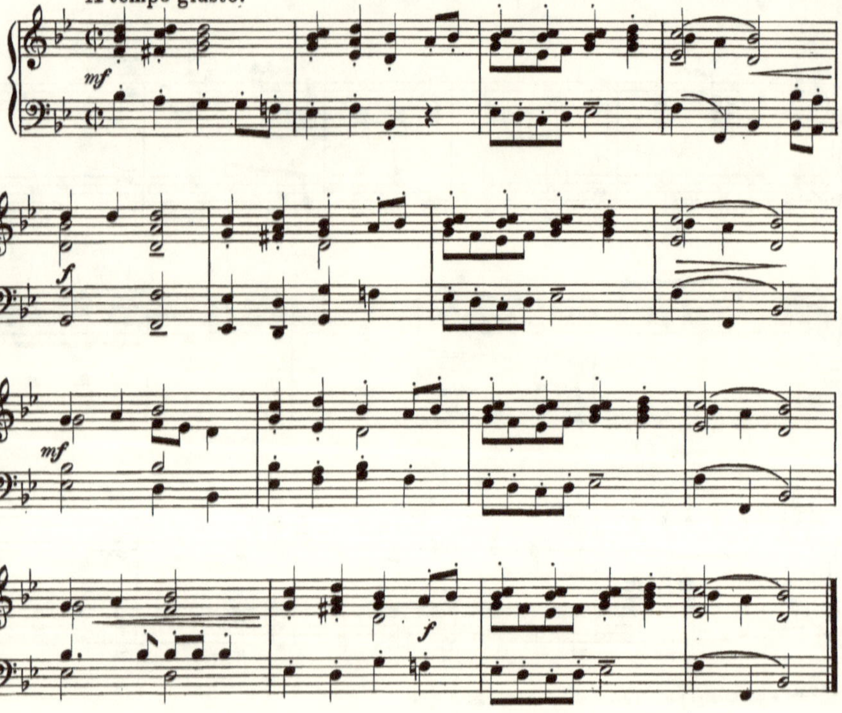

The May Pole.

COUNTRY DANCE.

Allegro moderato. *C. 1750.*

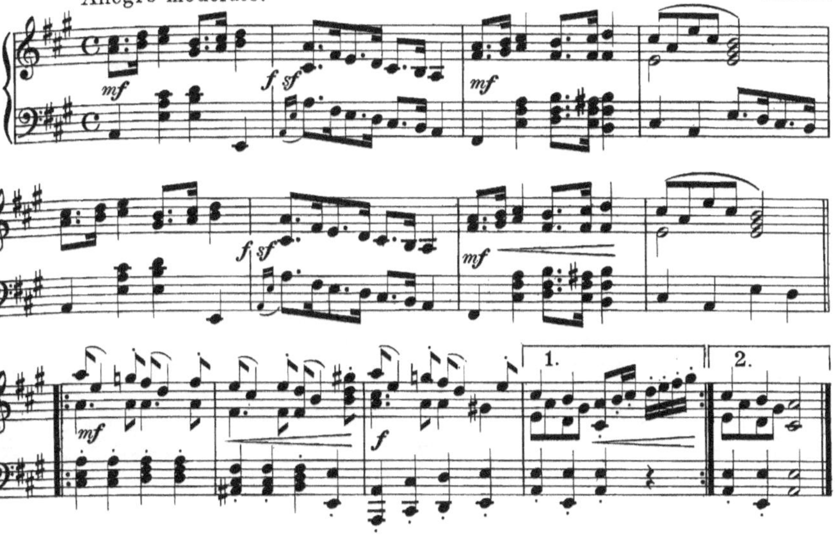

The Silver Box.

HORNPIPE.

Allegro vivo. *C. 1770.*

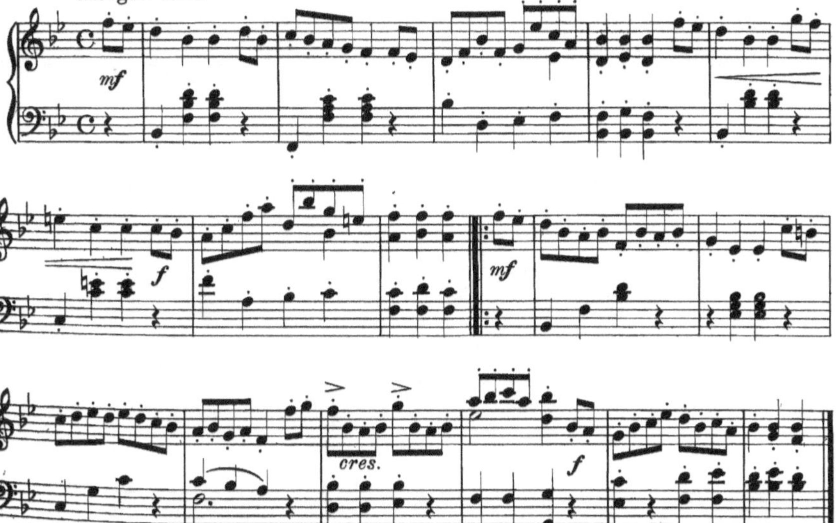

Le Bass.
BOURREE.

Late 17th century.

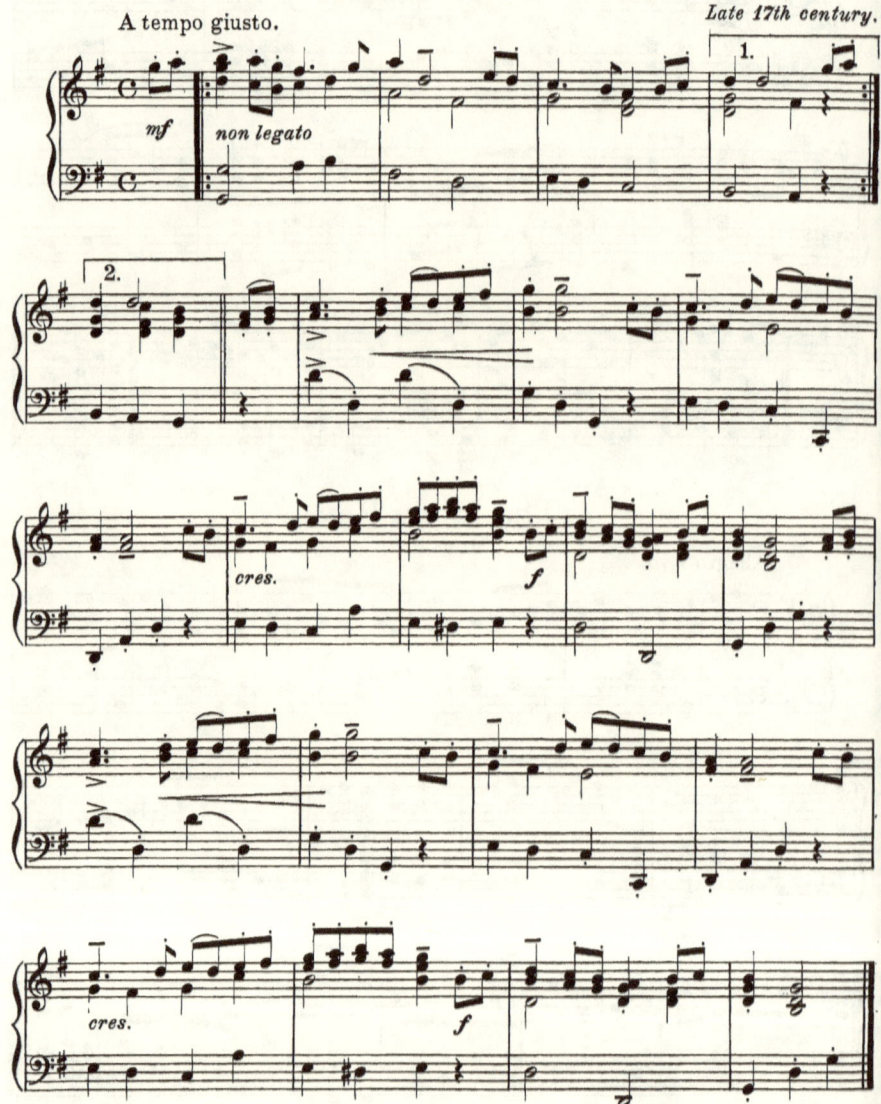

Kiss me early.

COUNTRY DANCE.

First half of 18th century.

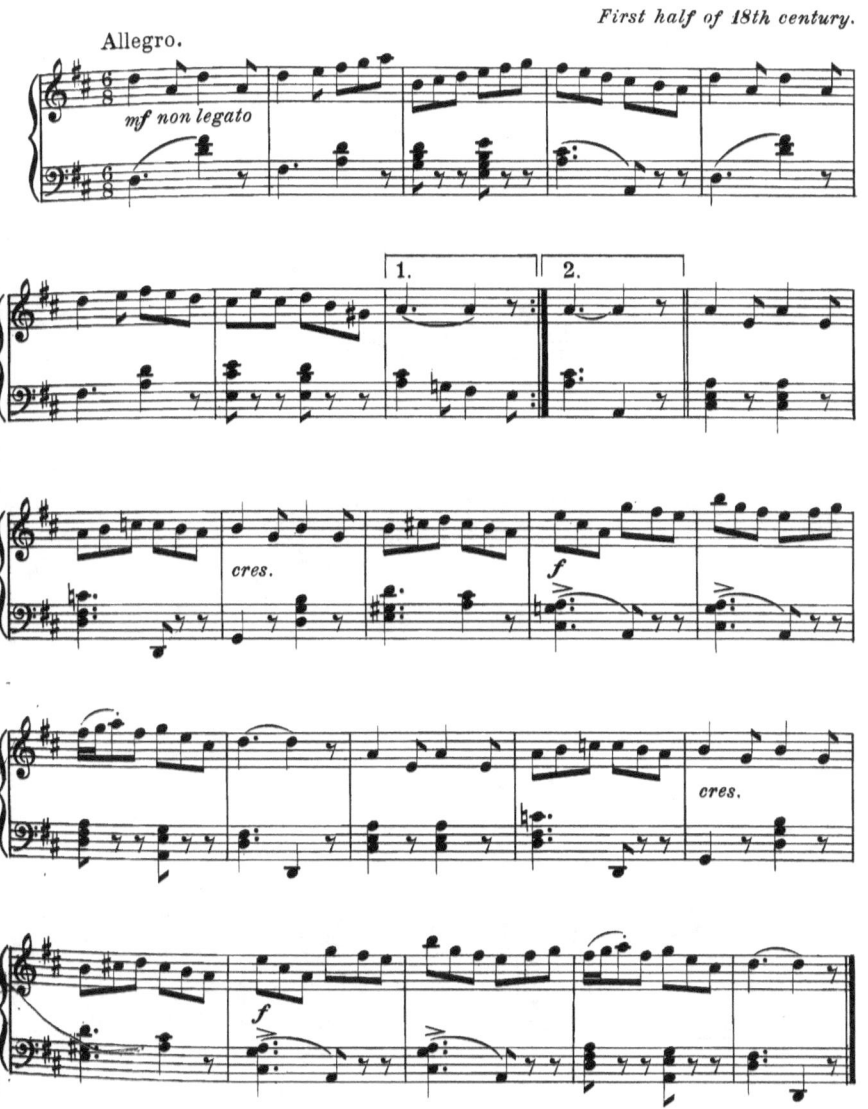

Cheshire Rounds.*

ROUND.

17th century.

Vivace.

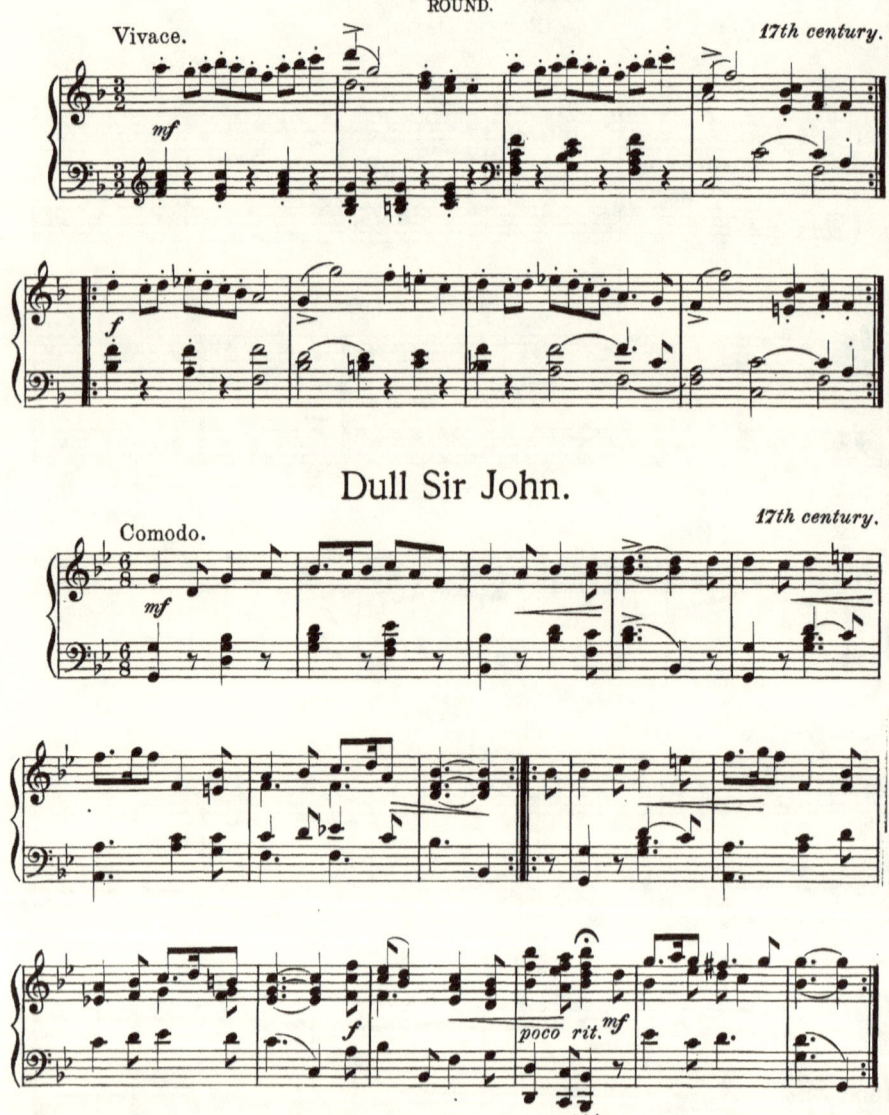

Dull Sir John.

17th century.

Comodo.

* This tune was played as a hornpipe in Thomas Doygett's play "The Country Wake" produced at Lincoln's Inn Field's Theatre in 1696. In 1711 it was printed in a collection of Country Dances for the Flute.

Miss Baker's Hornpipe.

Middle of 18th century.

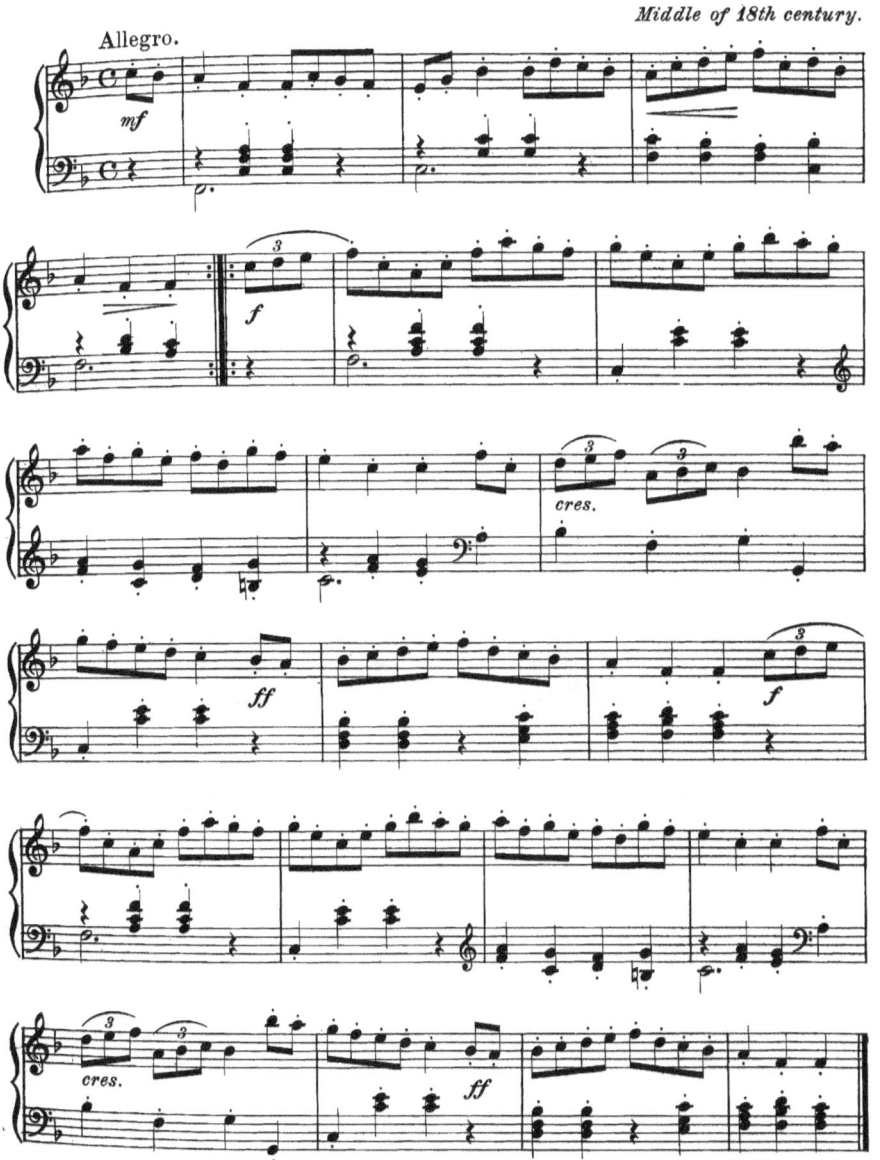

Lady Betty's Minuet.

Con grazia.

C. *1750*.

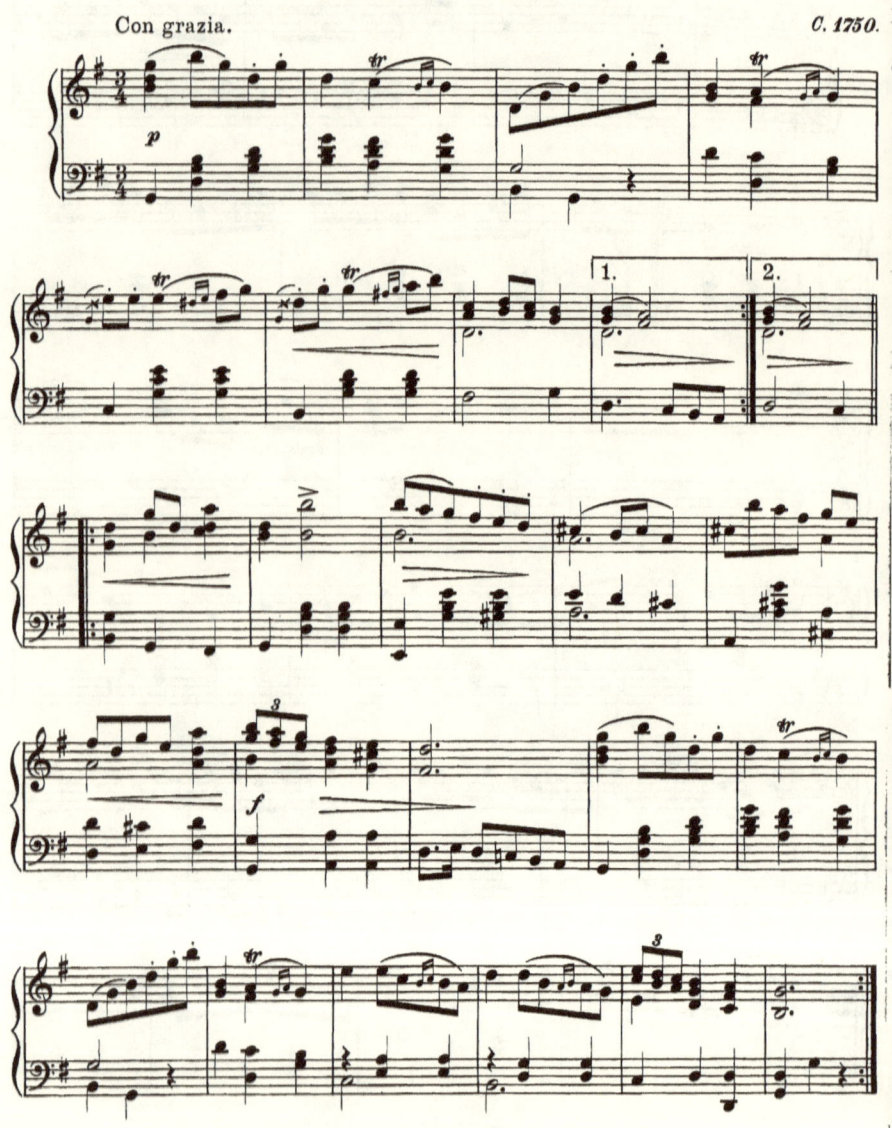

King James' March, or, The Garter.

Alla marcia.

Early 18th century

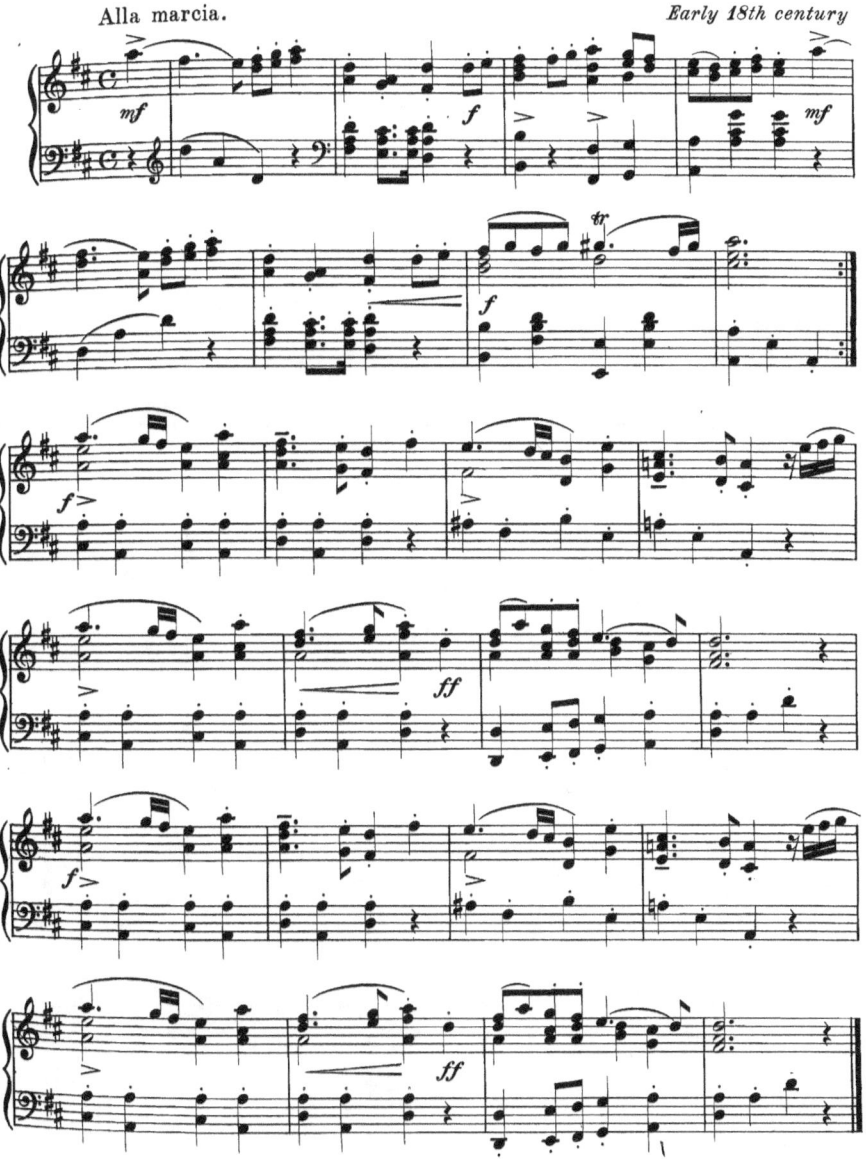

The Gold Ring.

COUNTRY DANCE.

Allegro ma non troppo.

Middle of 18th century

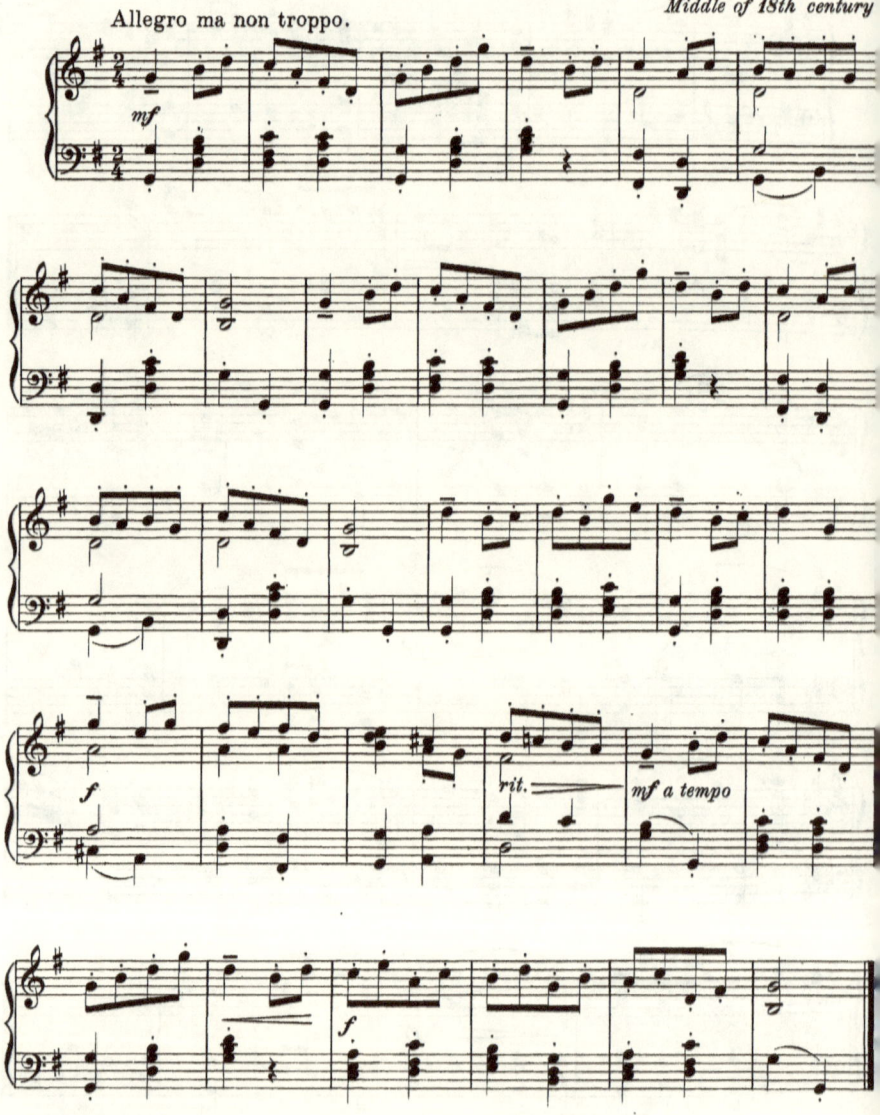

Princess Royal.*

MORRIS DANCE.

C. 1730.

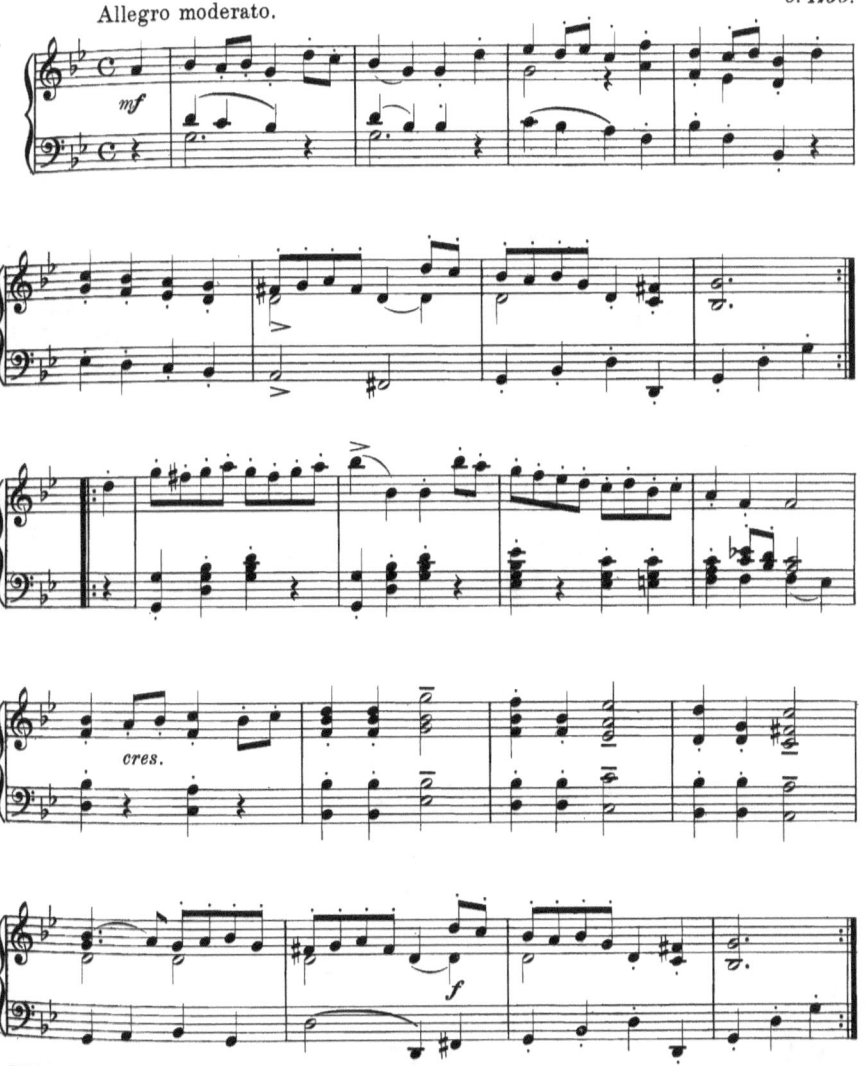

---

* This air has long been a favourite with Morris Dancers. Since the close of the 18th century it has been associated with Hoare's song "The Arethusa." Although difficult to determine its exact origin it is highly probable that "The Princess Royal" was composed by Carolan, the Irish harper. Authorities disagree, however on this point. Carolan was born in 1670 and died in 1788.

English Paspy.
(PASSEPIED.)

1711.

Ye Wild Morris.

C. 1720.

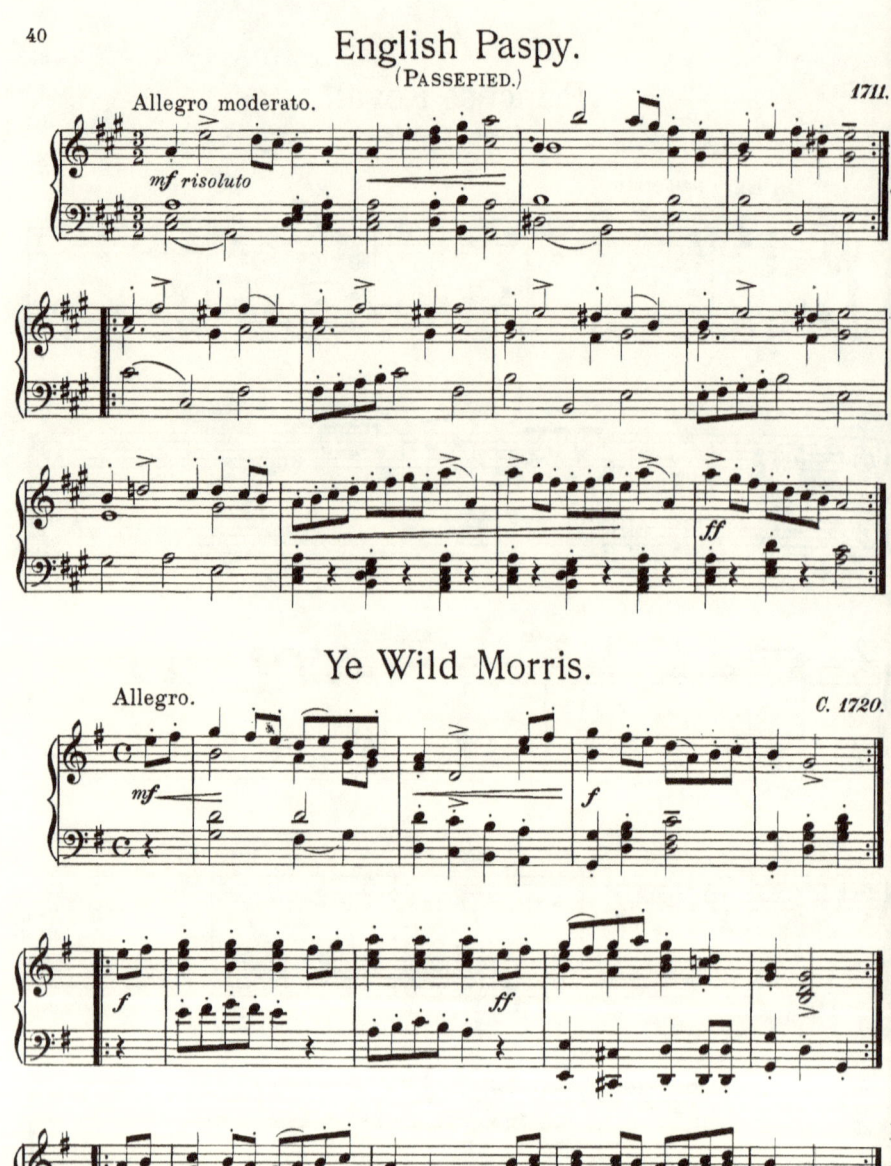

The Ship Hornpipe.

C. 1765.

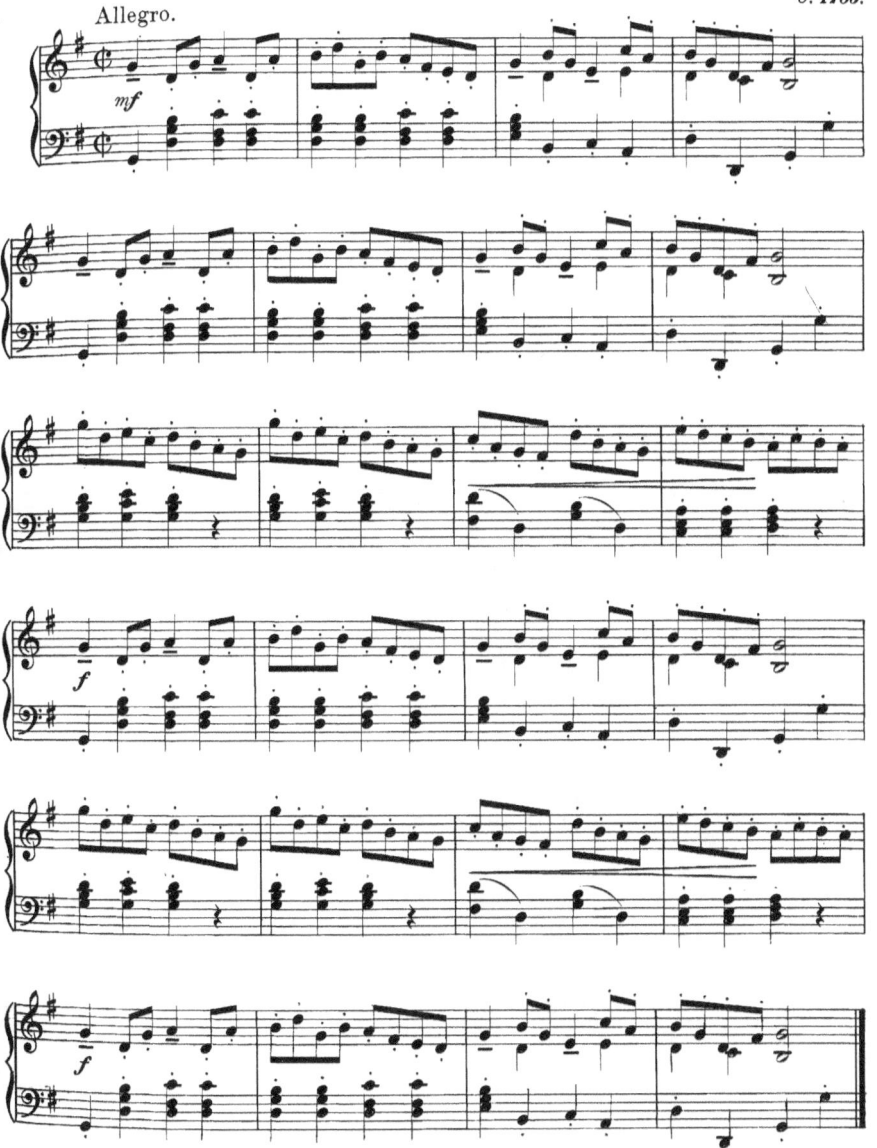

Harly Bush Fair.*

COUNTRY DANCE.

Allegretto.

C. 1750

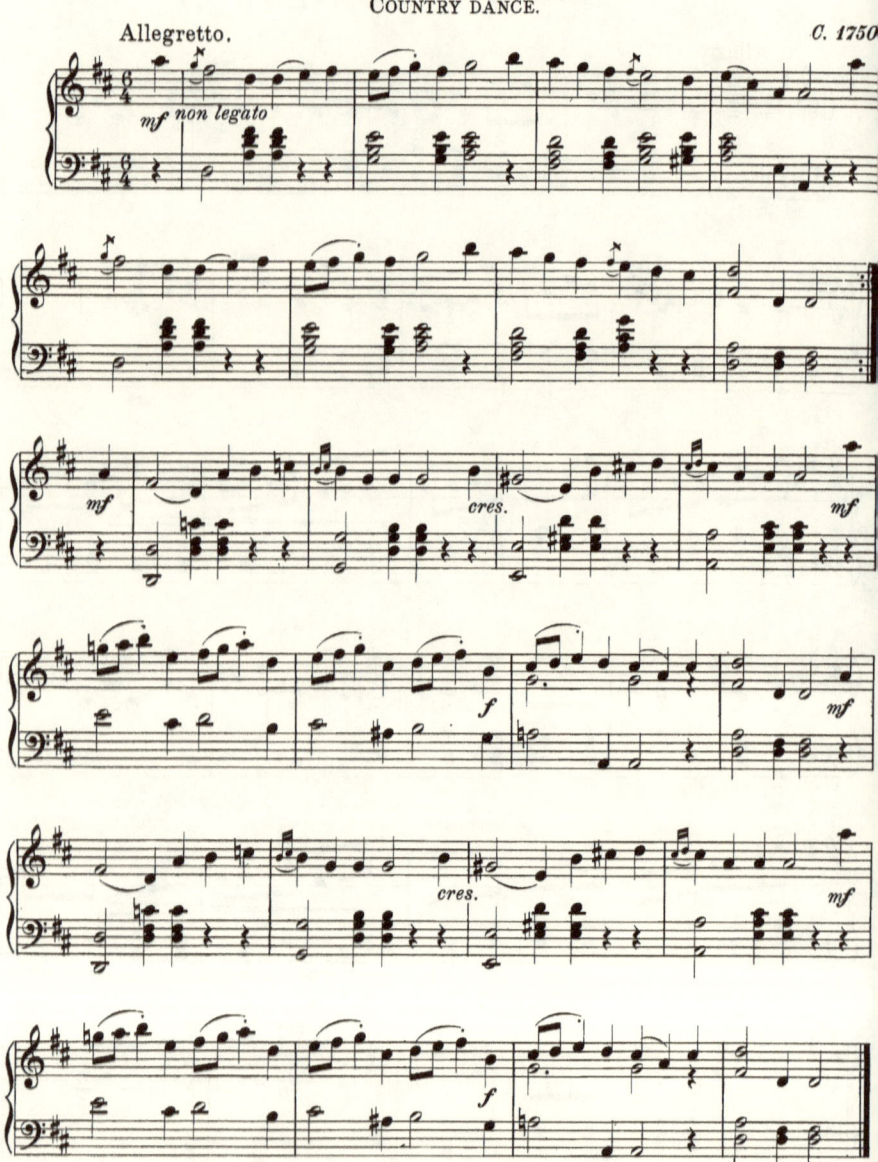

mf non legato

* This tune is the composition of an 18th century flautist of the name of Thomas Davis.

Kidlinton Green.

COUNTRY DANCE.

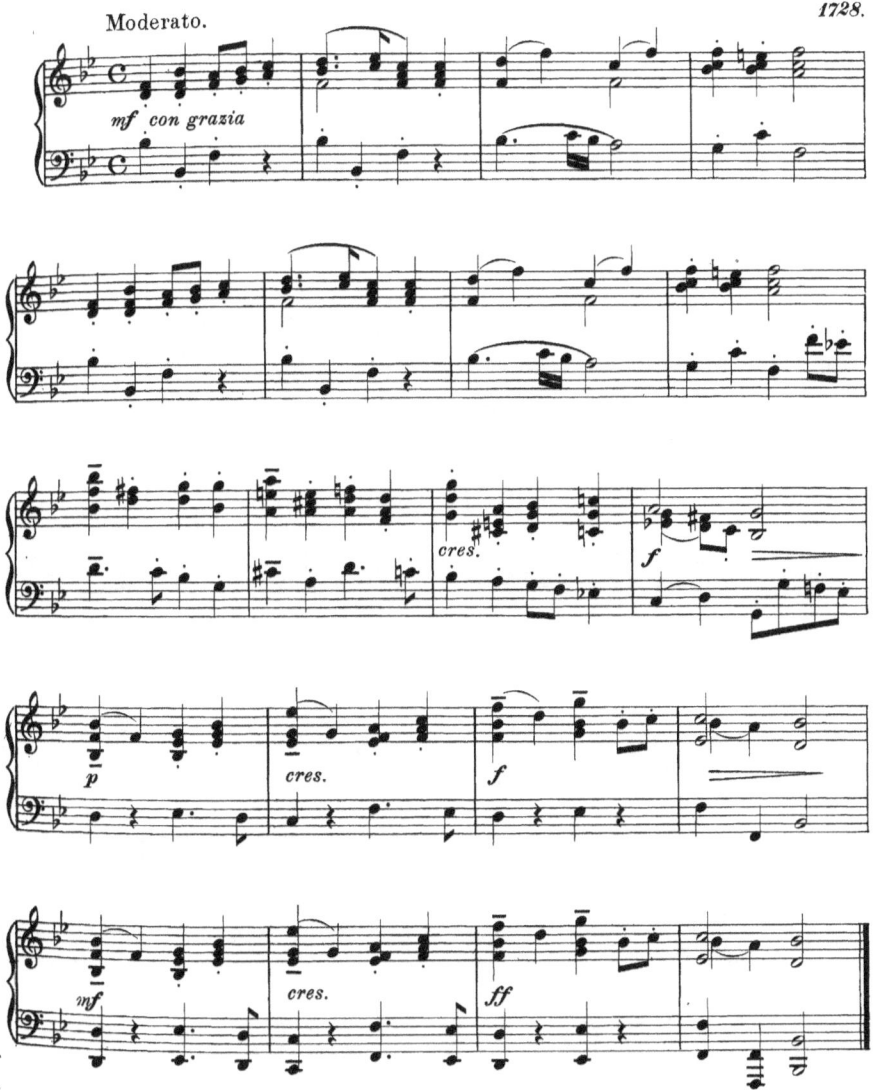

Collett's Jig.

C. 1750.

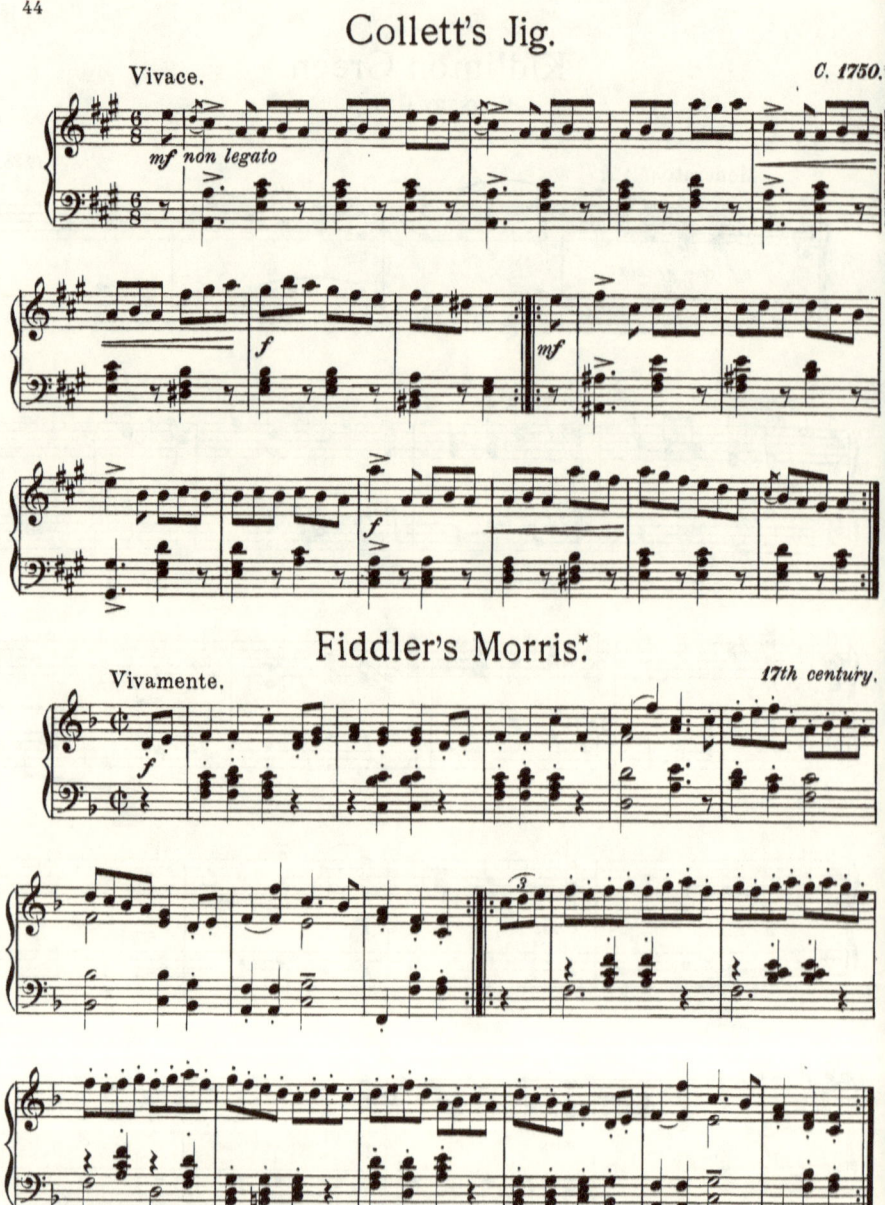

Fiddler's Morris.*

17th century.

*Known in Scotland as "O an ye were deid, guidman." It was for this tune that Burns wrote his song "There was a lad was born in Kyle."

Newmarket Downfall.

HORNPIPE.

C. *1765.*

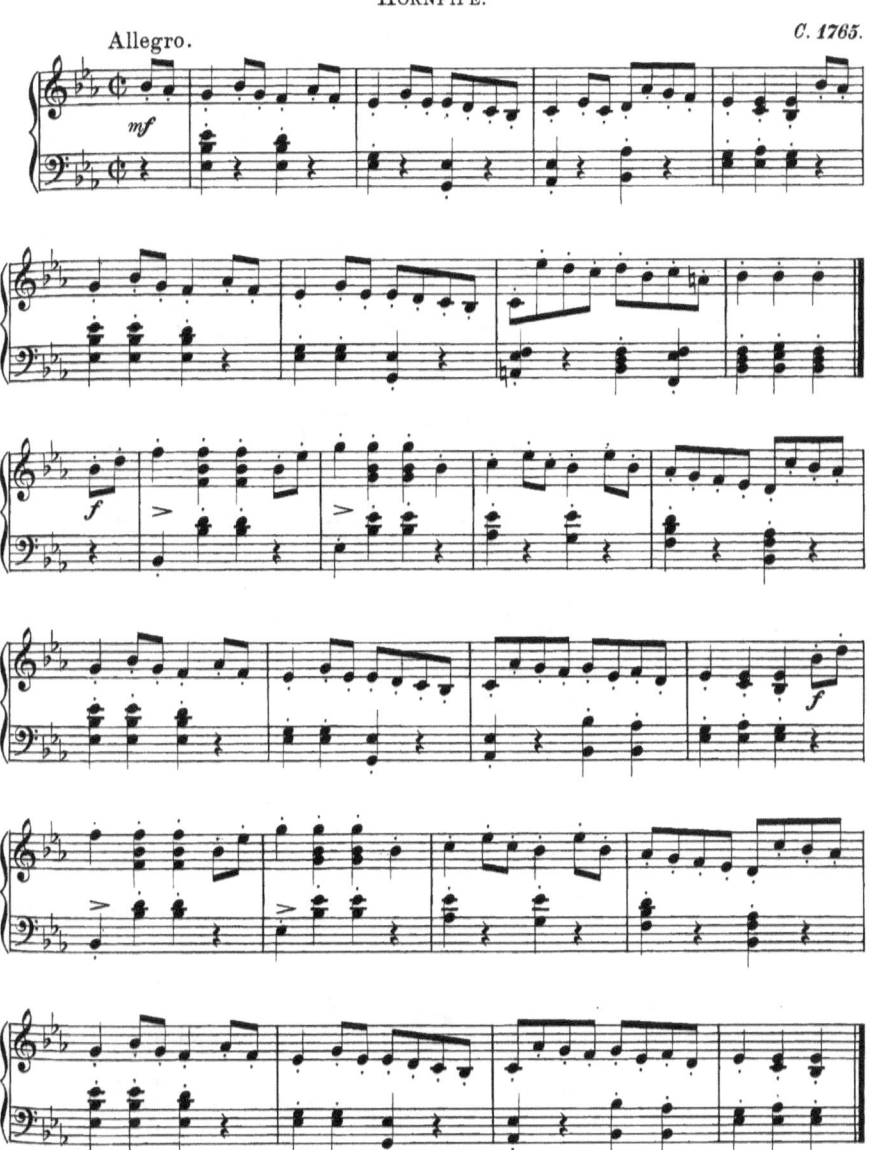

Miss Nancy frowns.

JIG.

St. James' Park.

Cotillion.

Allegro vivamente.

C. 1780.

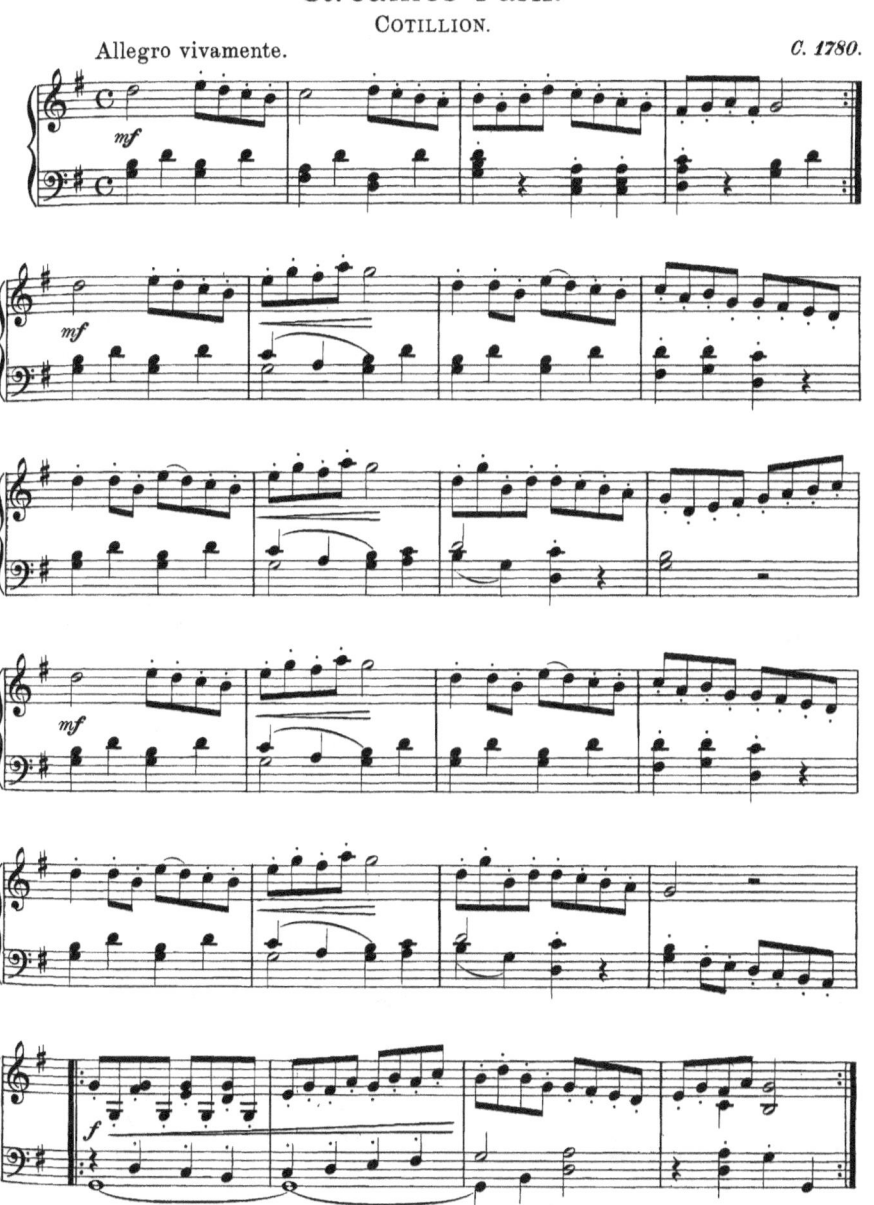

Dargason or The Sidany.

COUNTRY DANCE.

17th Century.

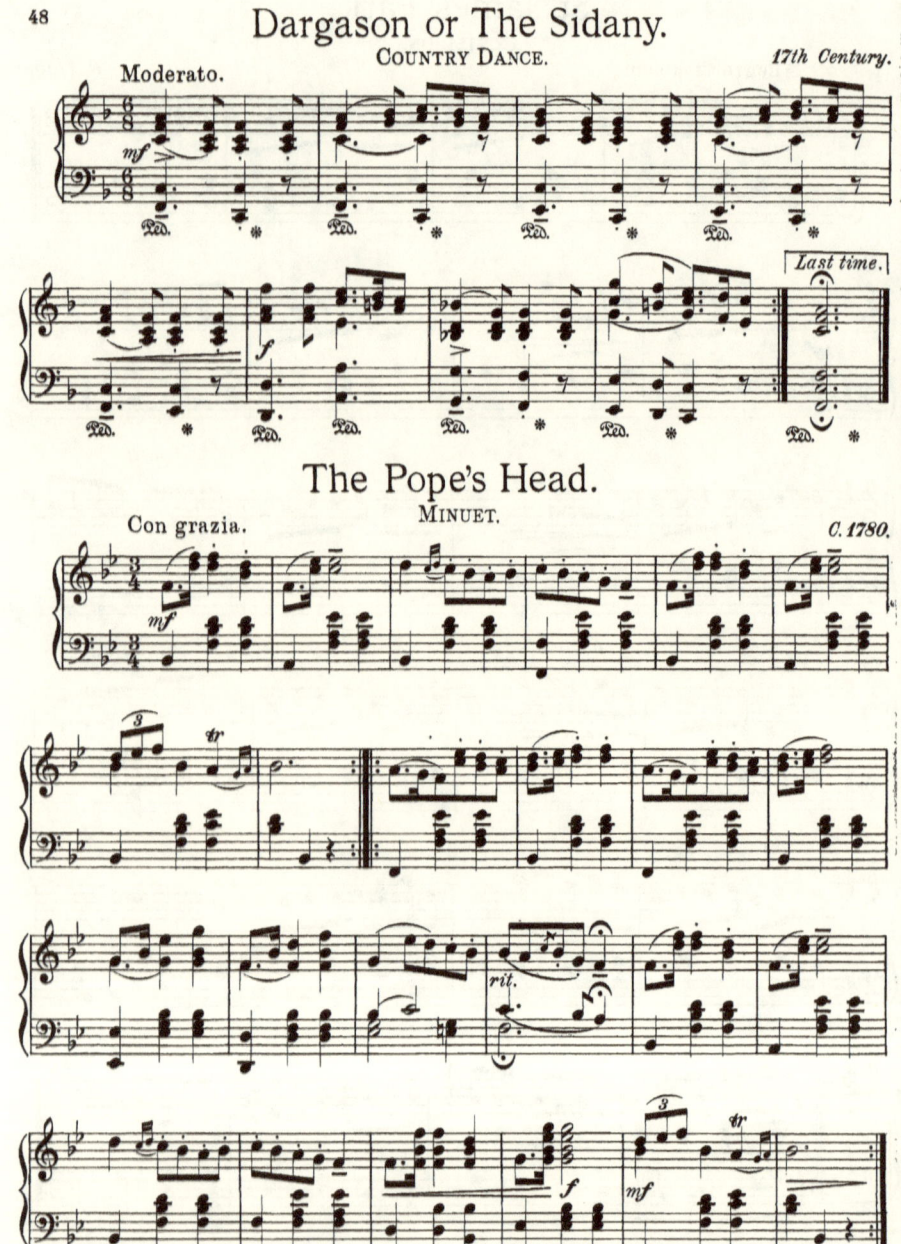

The Pope's Head.

MINUET.

C. 1780.

Sir Roger de Coverley.

COUNTRY DANCE.

1685.

Con spirito.

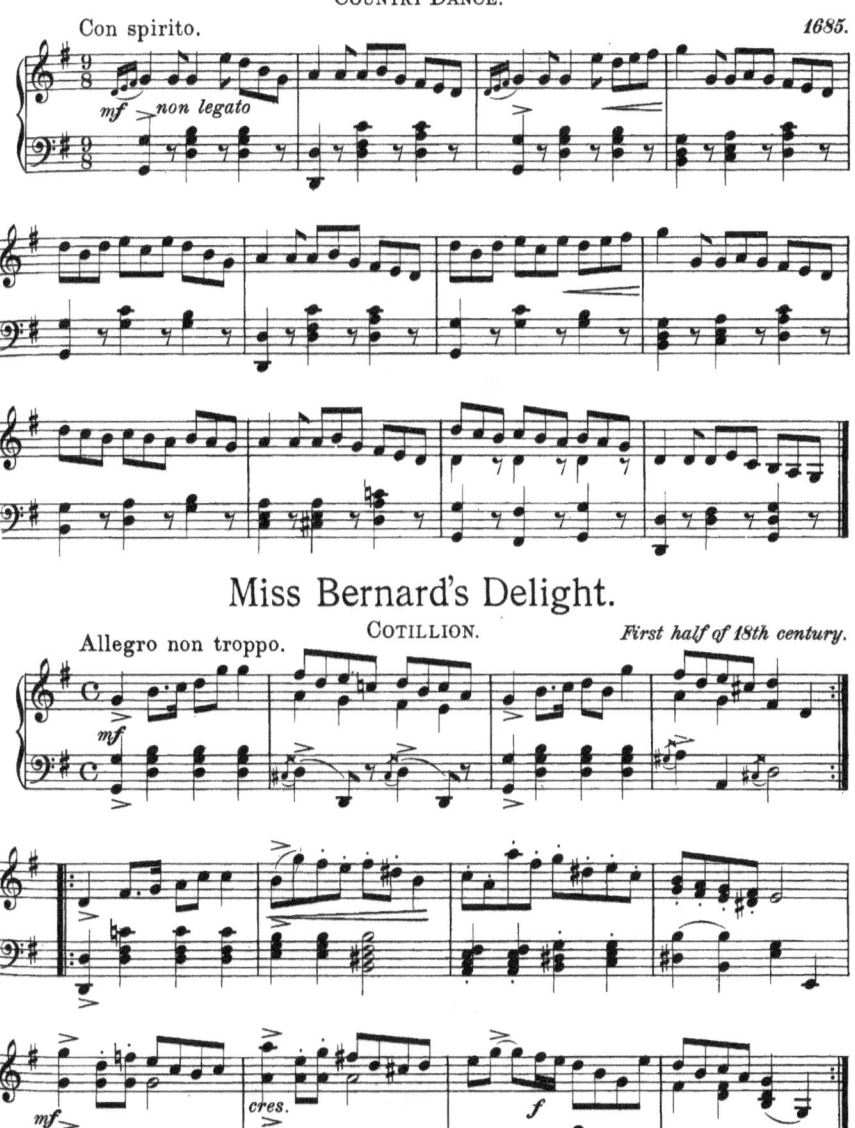

Miss Bernard's Delight.

COTILLION.

Allegro non troppo.

First half of 18th century.

50

Helston Furry Dance.*
MORRIS DANCE.

Moderato ma molto risoluto.

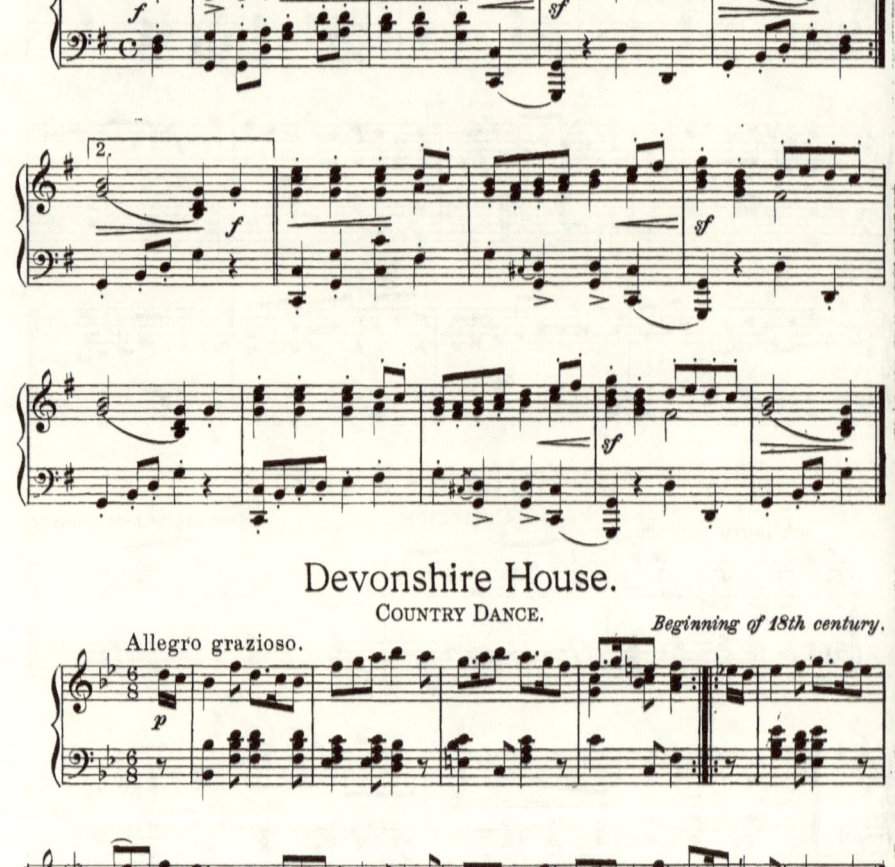

Devonshire House.
COUNTRY DANCE.

Beginning of 18th century.

Allegro grazioso.

---

* Although not printed until the beginning of the 19th century this is evidently a genuinely ancient Morris dance tune. It has much in common with "A Morris Dance" (p. 22,) which is preserved in Wright's *Pleasant and Merry Humours* c. 1720.

New Boree.

BOUREE.

Moderato enfatico.

Early 18th century.

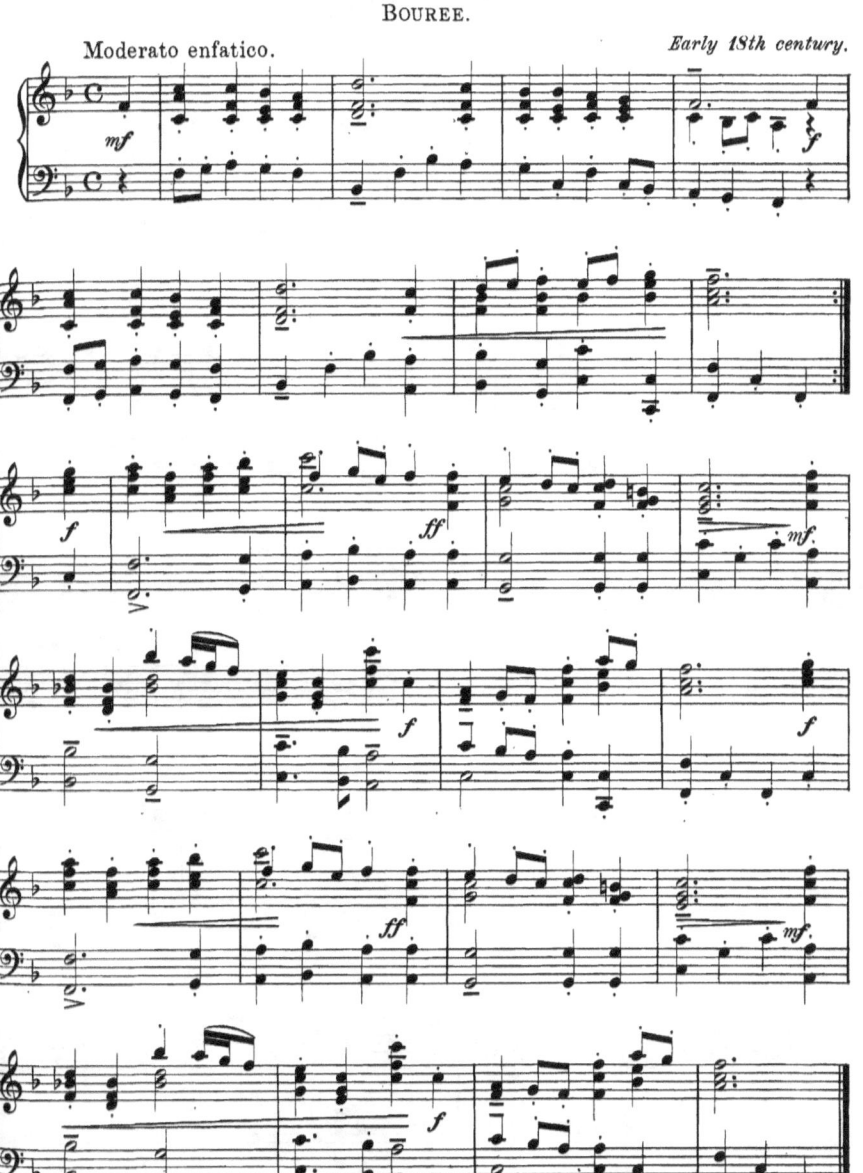

Saraband.*

Lento con risoluzione.

17th century.

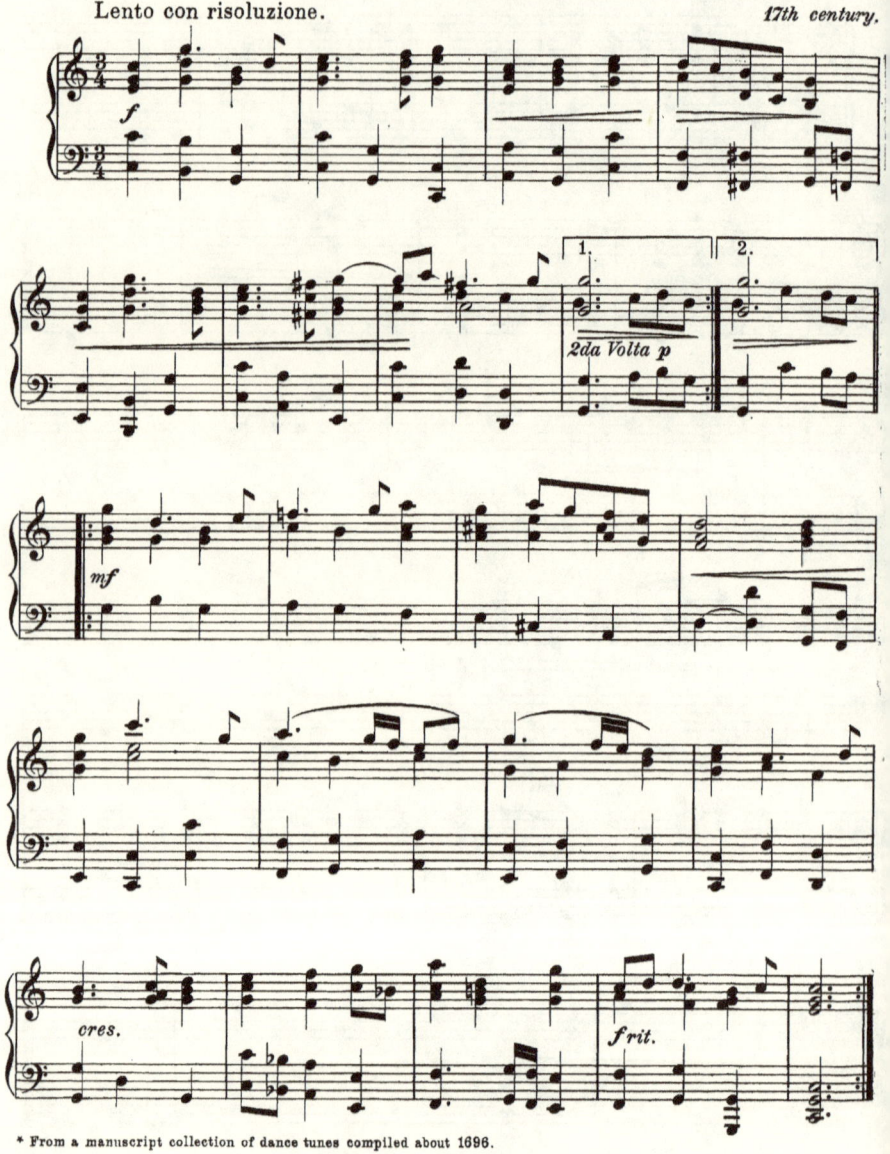

* From a manuscript collection of dance tunes compiled about 1696.

Duke of Marlborough's Health.

MARCH.

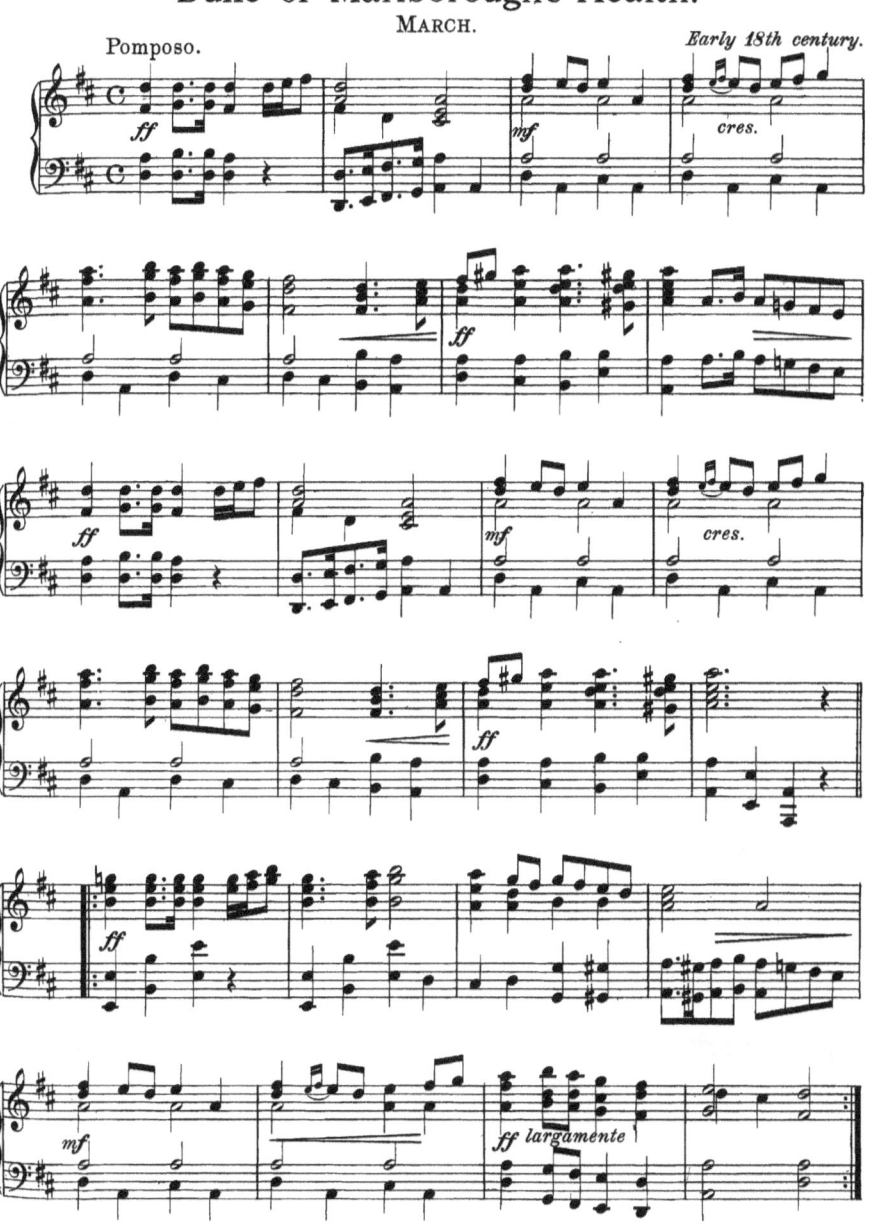

Danny.

COUNTRY DANCE.

Con spirito.

First half of 18th century.

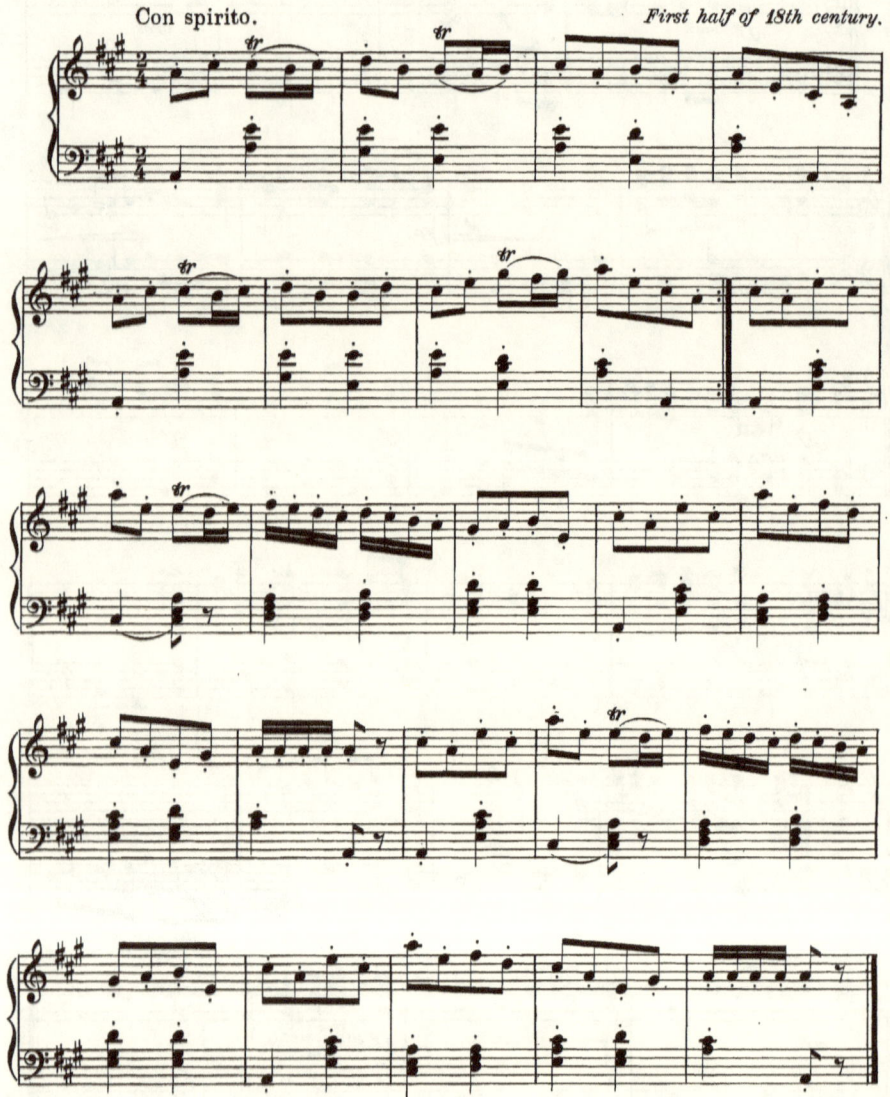

A Paspy.

(Passepied.)

Early 18th century.

Con spirito.

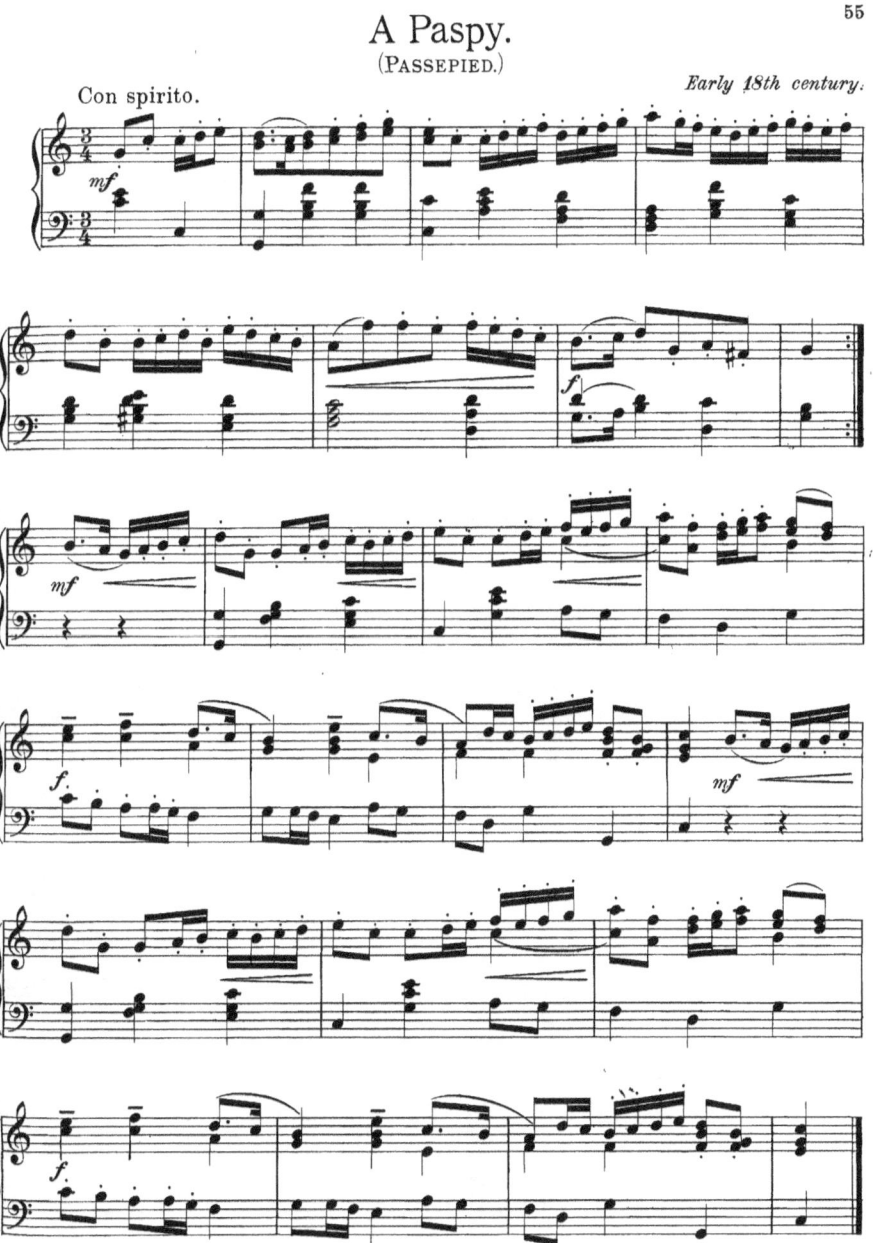

Will o' the Wisp.

COUNTRY DANCE.

Allegro ma non troppo.

First half of 18th century.

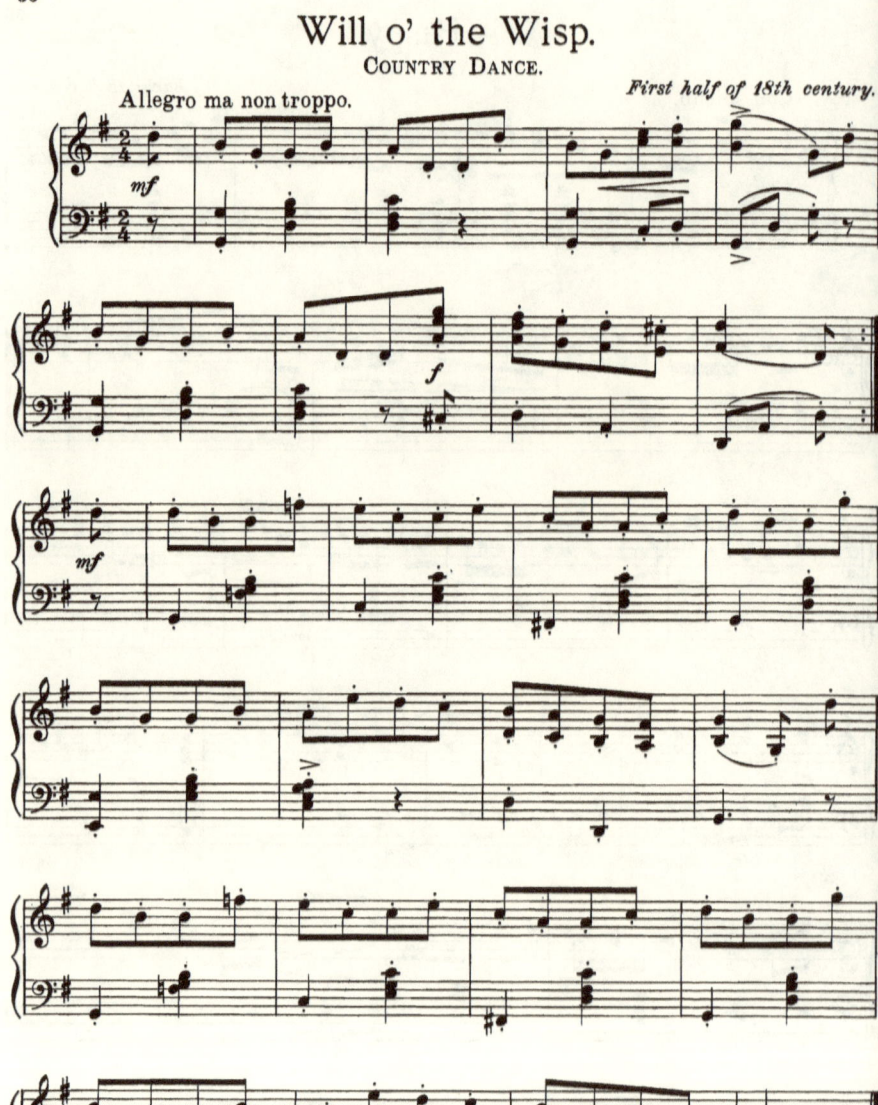

Chelsea Reach or Buckingham House.

COUNTRY DANCE.

17th century.

Moderato con grazio.

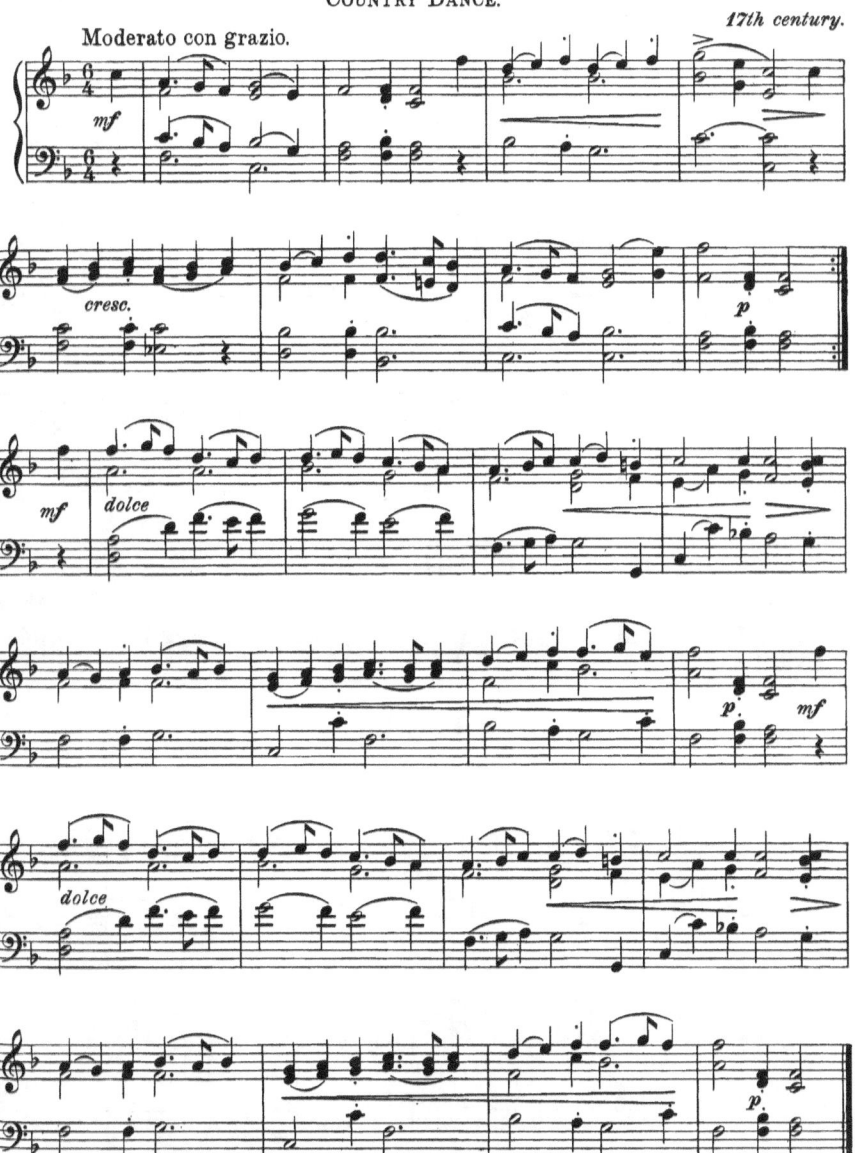

58

Blacksmith's Morris.

C. 1720.

Allegro moderato.

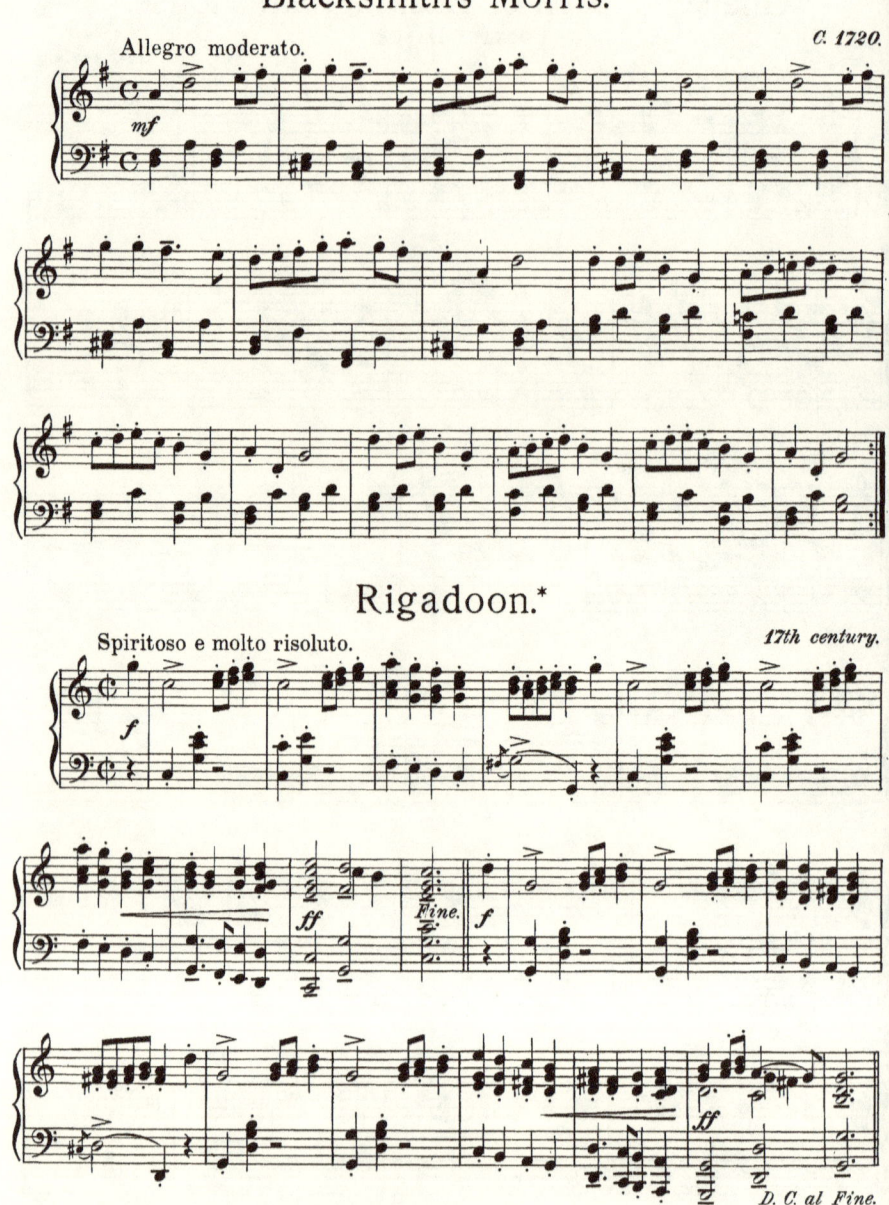

Rigadoon.*

Spiritoso e molto risoluto.

17th century.

D. C. al Fine.

* From a Manuscript collection of Dance tunes compiled about 1690.

Cockle Shells.

MORRIS DANCE.

1701.

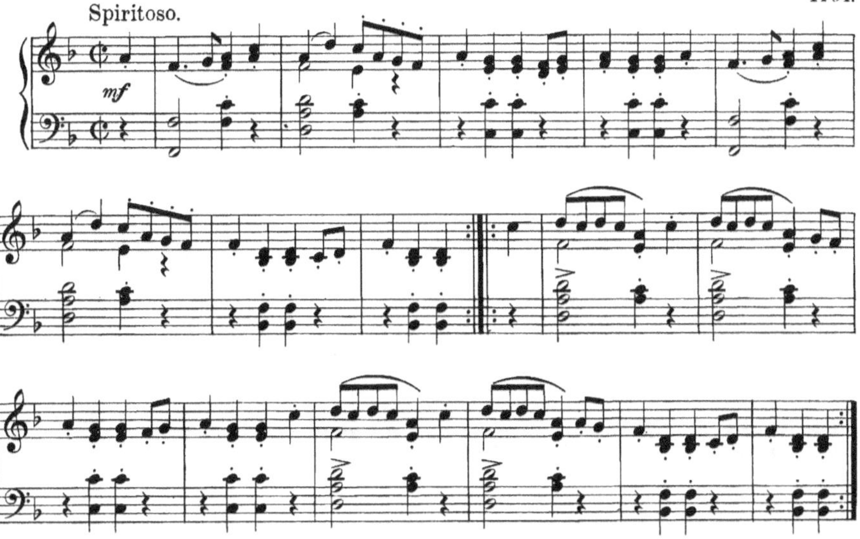

Spiritoso.

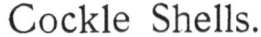

Tunbridge Frisk.

COUNTRY DANCE.

C. 1745.

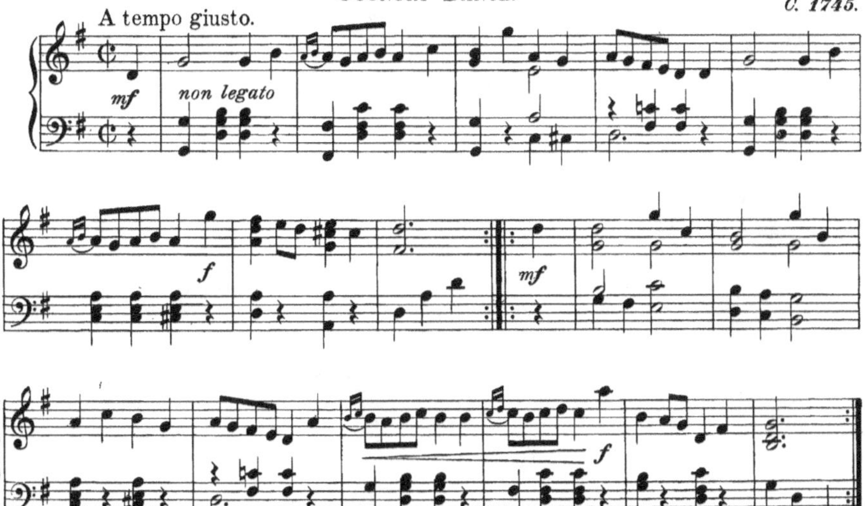

A tempo giusto.

mf *non legato*

Known in Scotland as "The Highland Laddie."

Up and Down.

COUNTRY DANCE.

C. 1770.

Allegro ma non troppo.

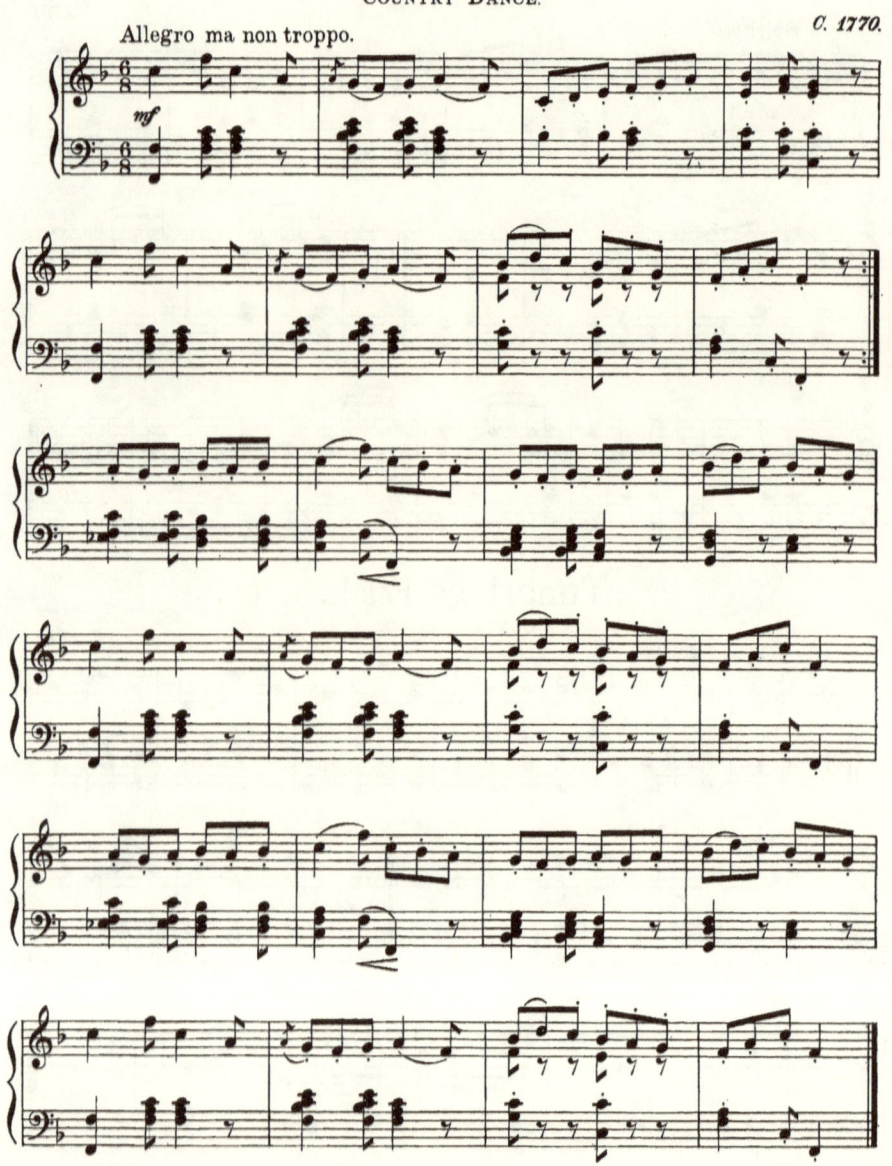

La Foes.

ALLEMAND.

1775.

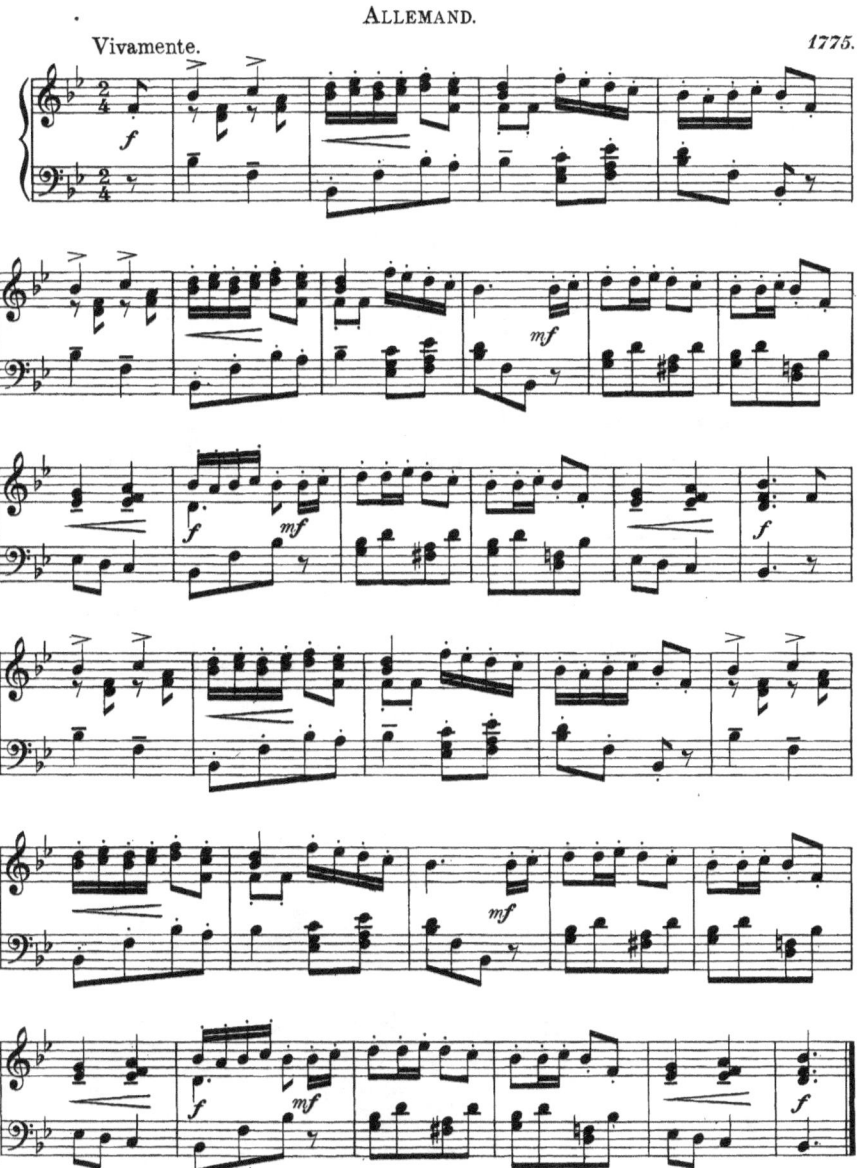

Peggy Perkins.

C. 1780.

Poco Allegro.

The Prague Minuet.

Middle of 18th century.

Con grazia.

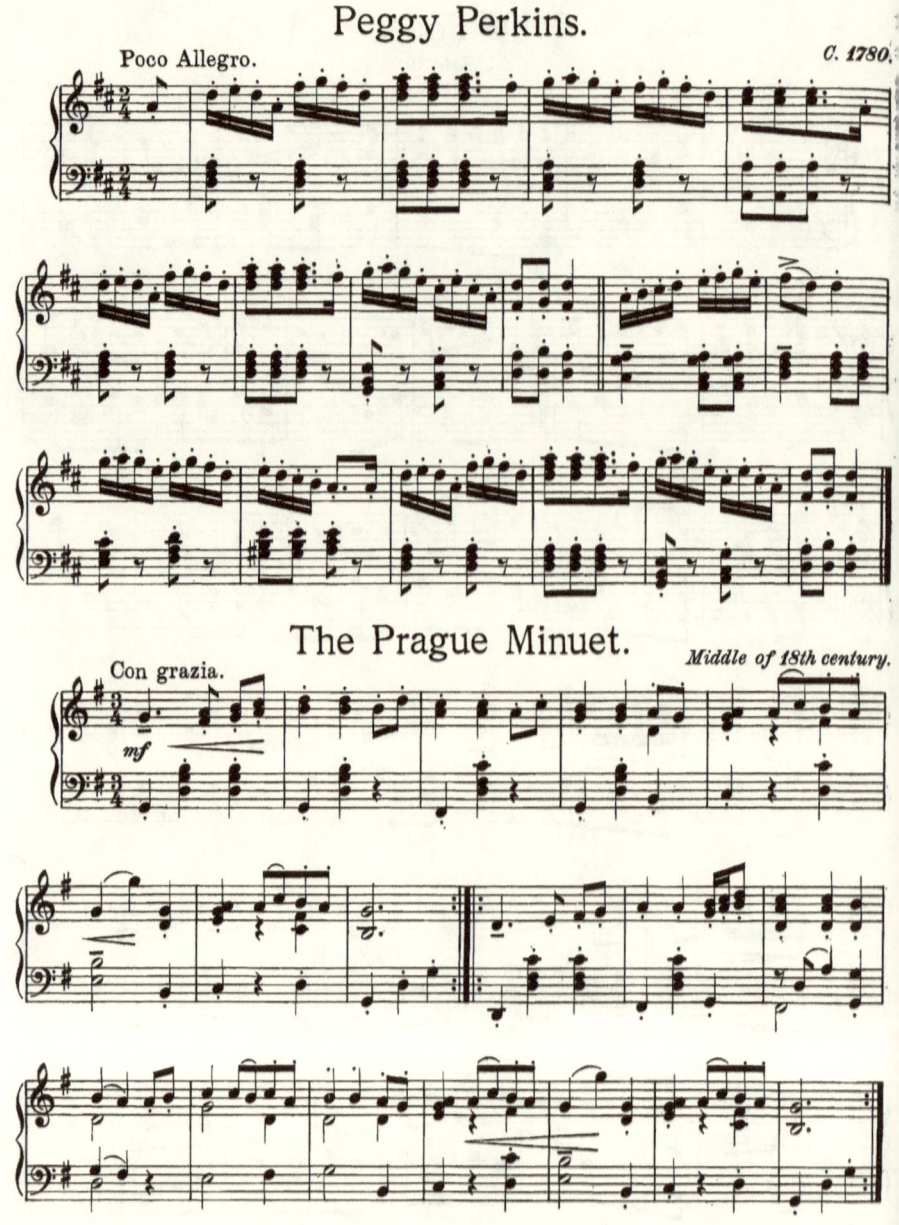

Kew Green.
JIG.

C. 1750.

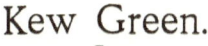

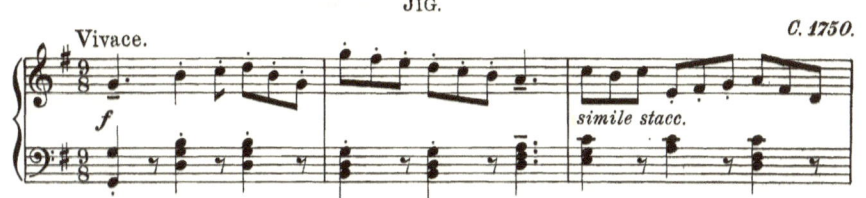

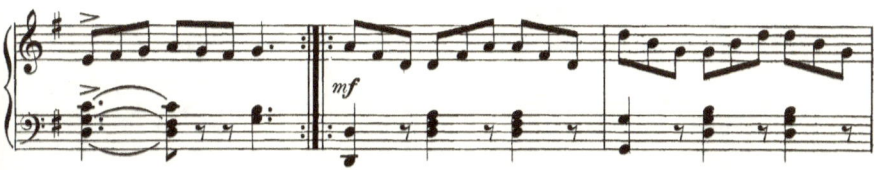

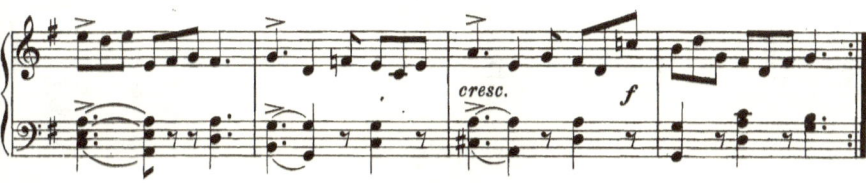

The Maids.
COUNTRY DANCE.

C. 1720.

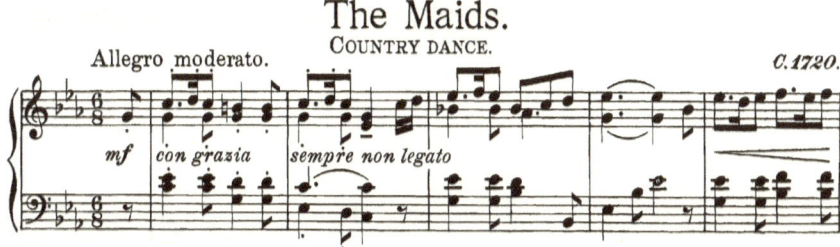

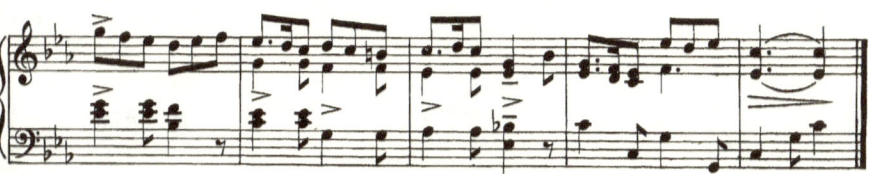

64

Belvediere.
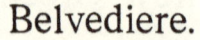
COTILLION.

C. 1780

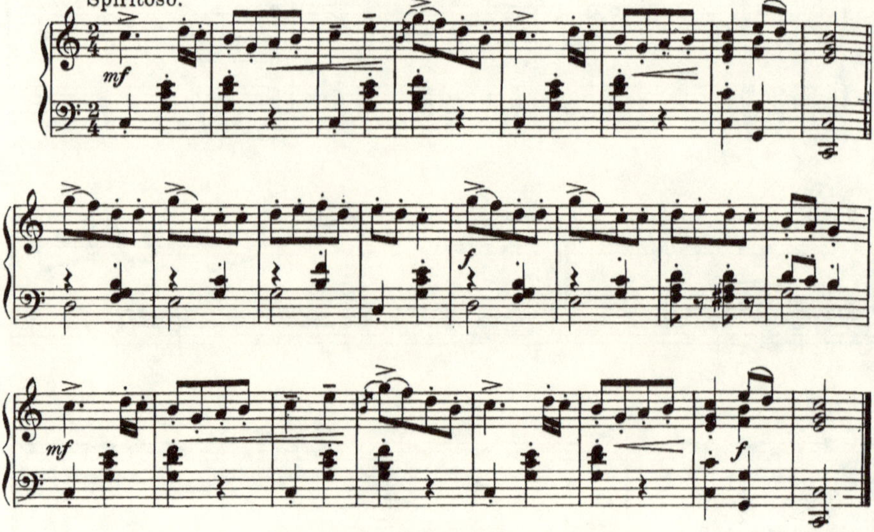

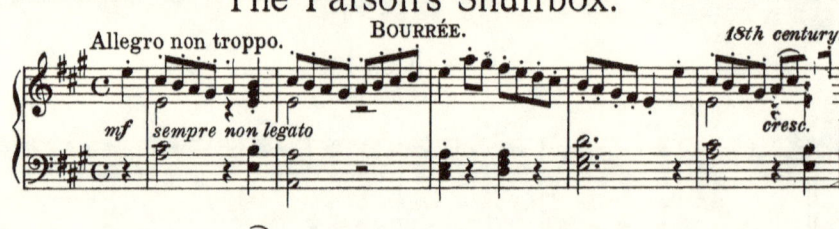

The Parson's Snuffbox.
BOURRÉE.

18th century.

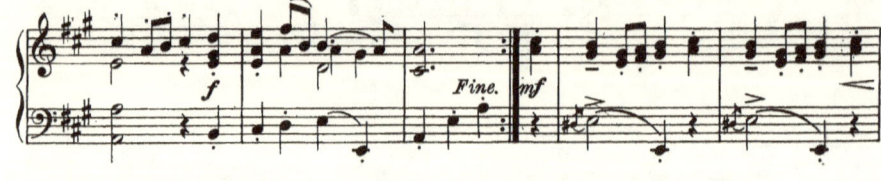

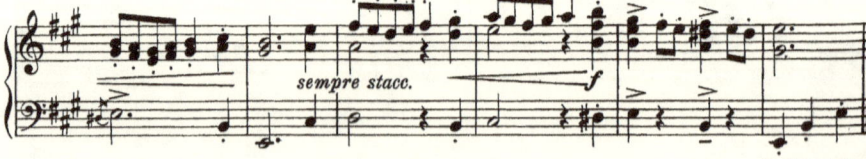

D. C. al Fine.

Parson and Dorothy.

COUNTRY DANCE.

Early 18th century.

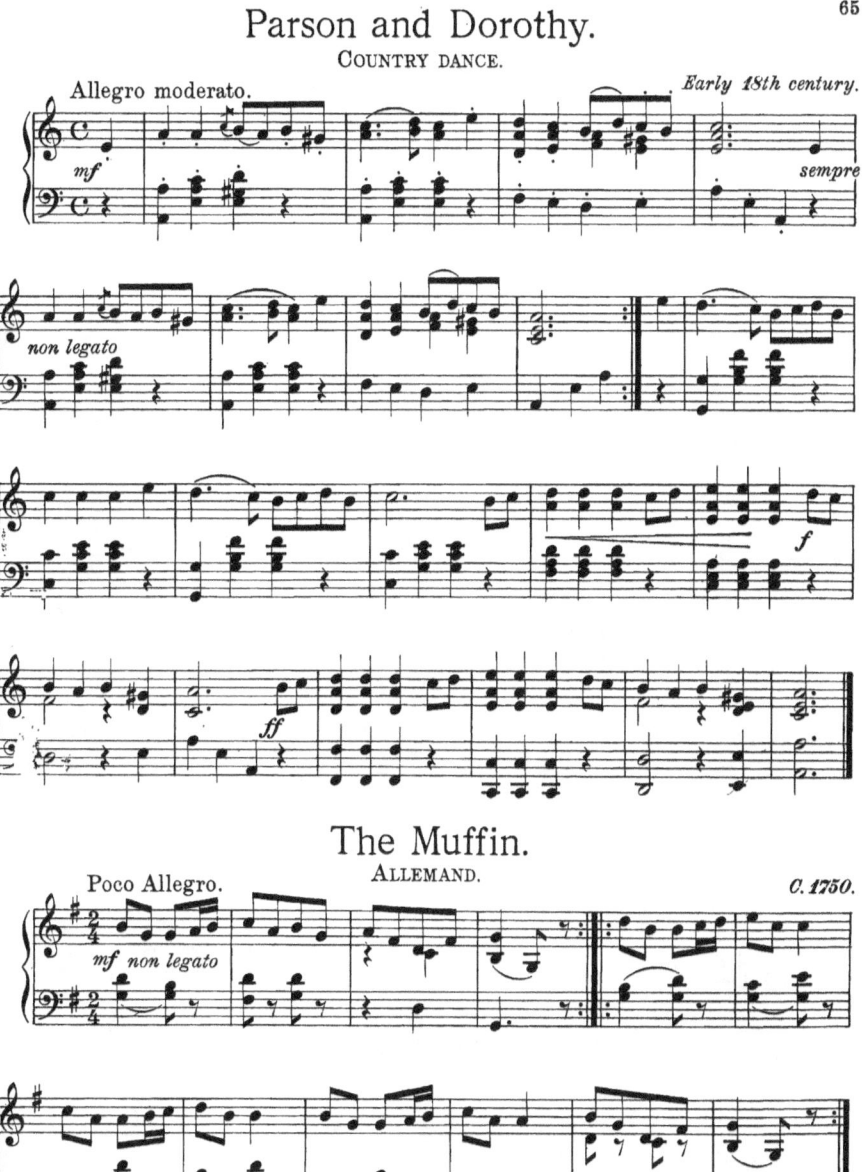

The Muffin.

ALLEMAND.

C. 1750.

Miss Loames' Minuet.

C. 1750.

Con grazia.

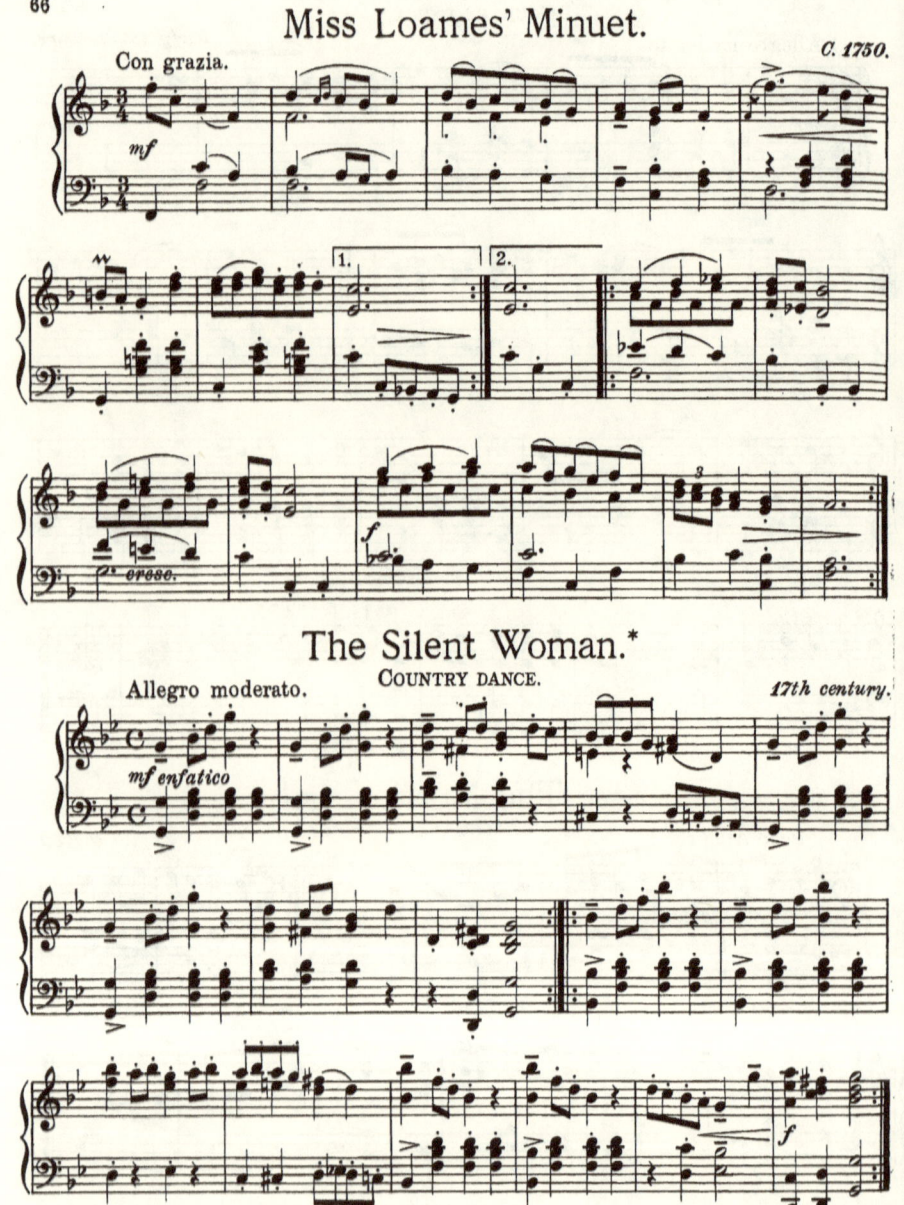

The Silent Woman.*

COUNTRY DANCE.

Allegro moderato.

17th century.

*This dance was introduced in the play "The Silent Woman" produced in London towards the close of the 17th century.

La Belle Catherine.

ALLEMAND.

C.1780.

Kitty Fisher.

COUNTRY DANCE.

Middle of 18th century.

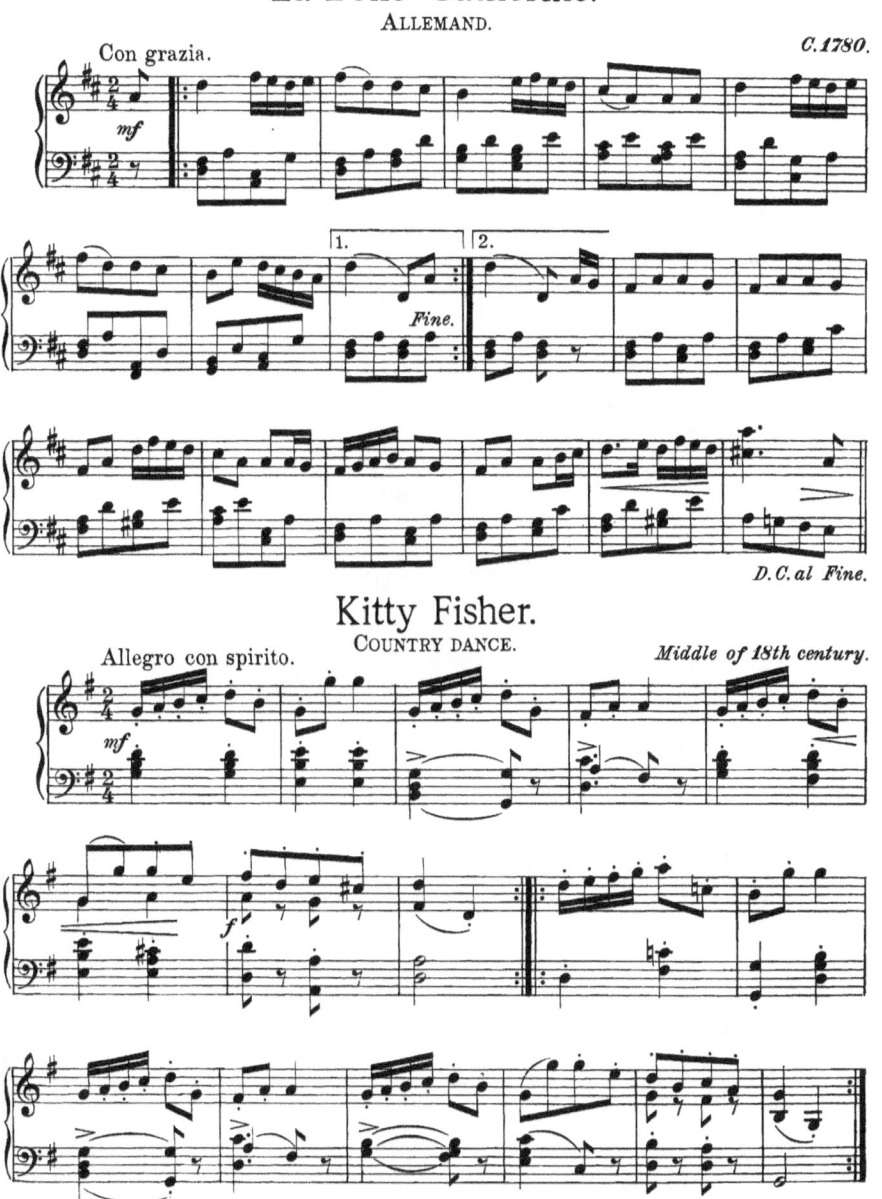

The Wedding Ring.

COTILLION.

Vivamente.

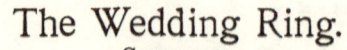

End of 18th century.

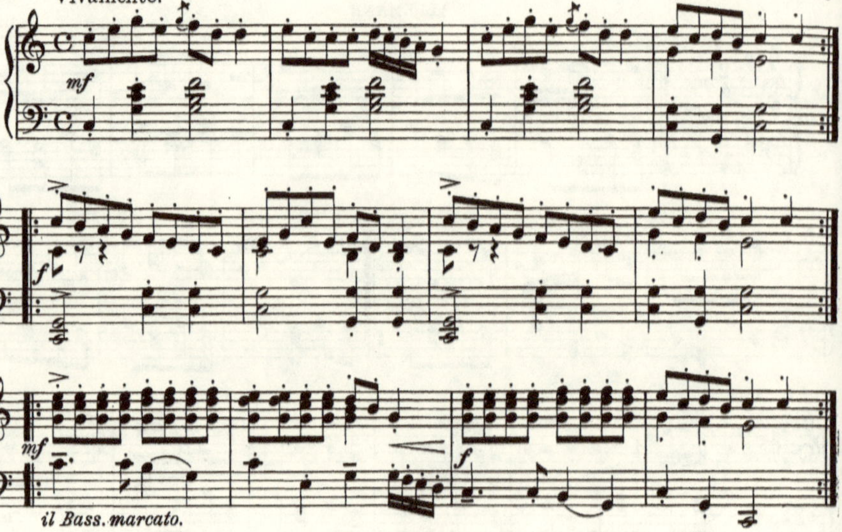

mf

f

mf

il Bass. marcato.

The Chaplet.

GAVOTTE.

C. 1740.

Con grazia.

mf

dim.

tr

f

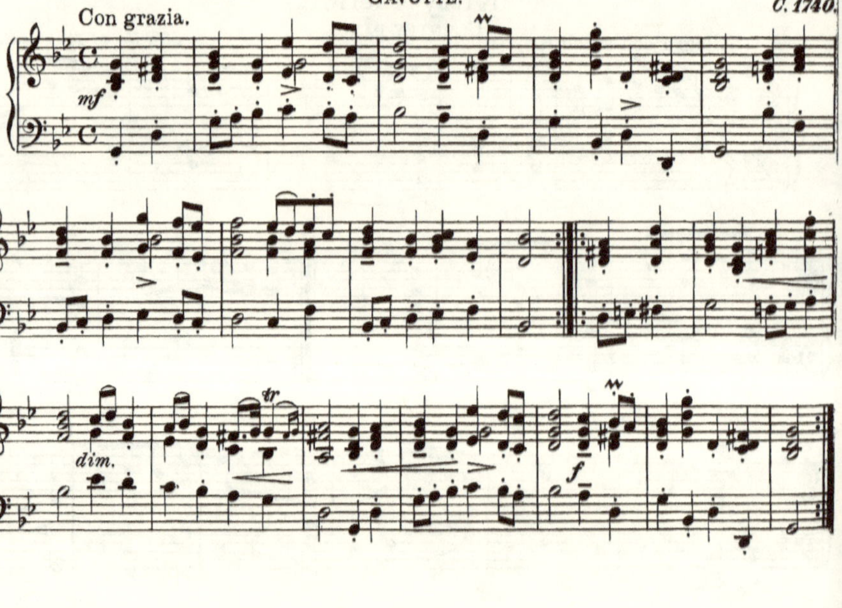

La Pavane.

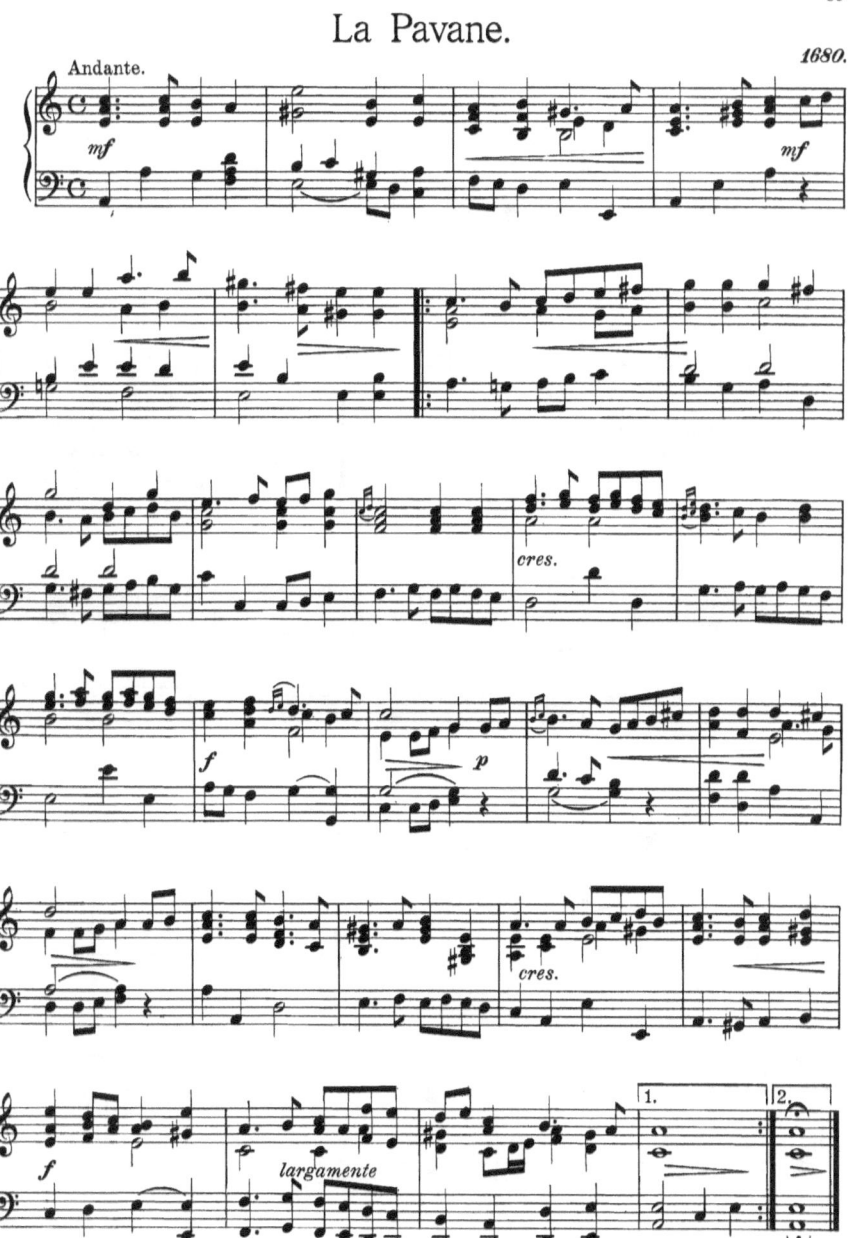

Gaillarde.

LA ROMANESCA.

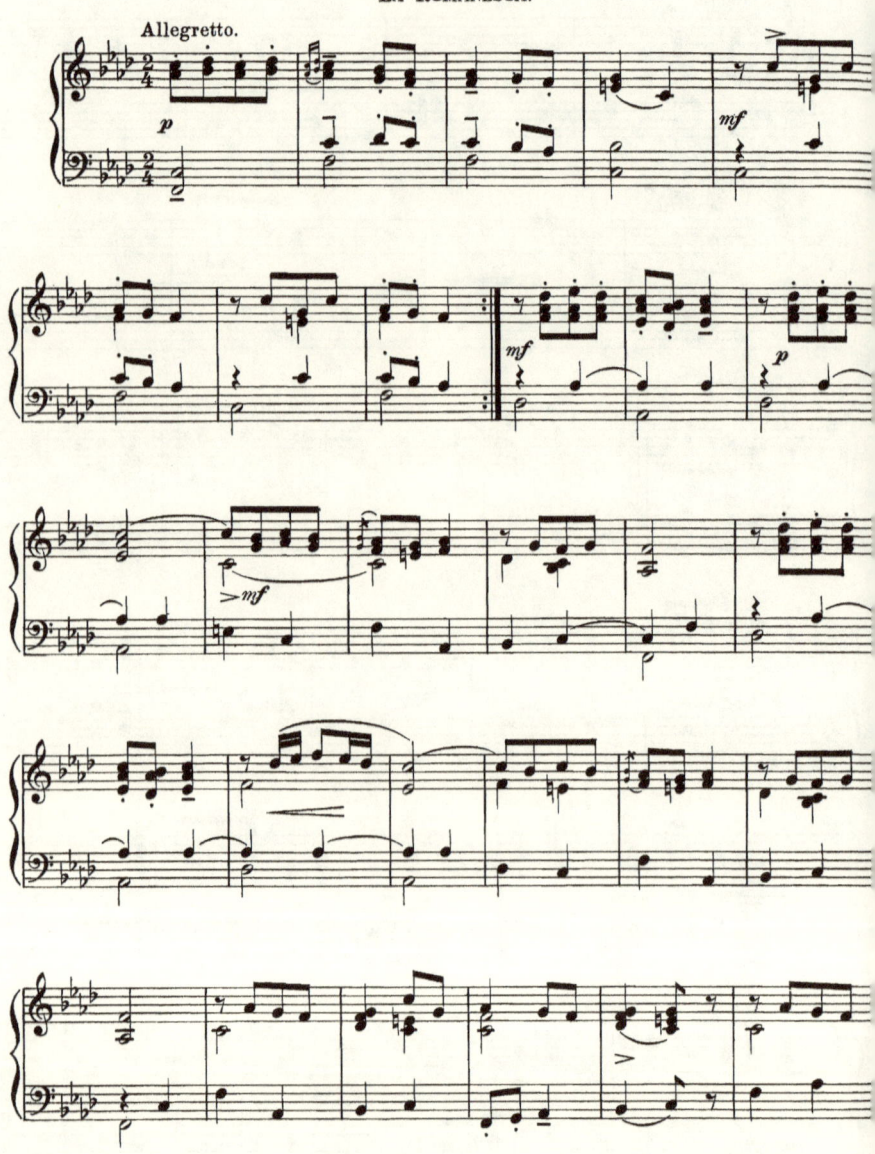

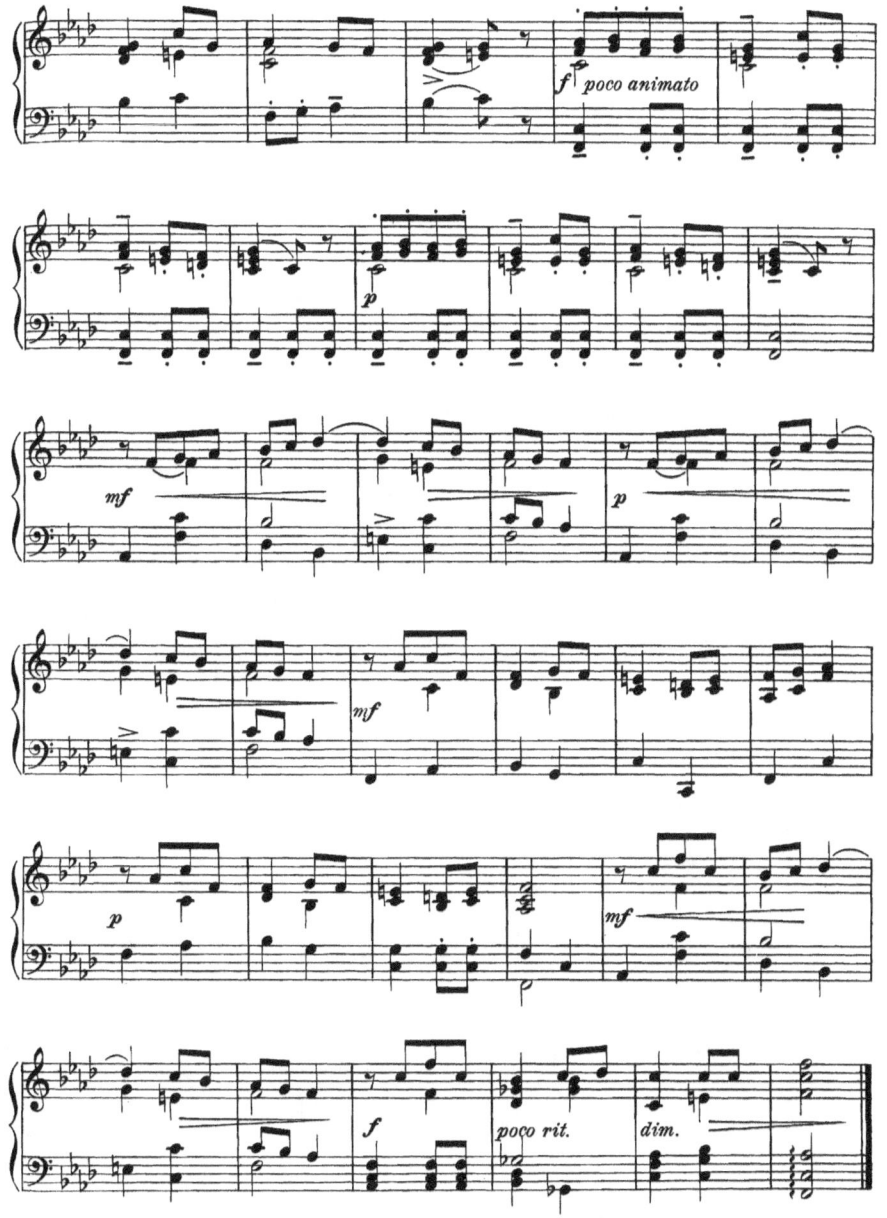

Courante.

1715.

Allegro con energio.

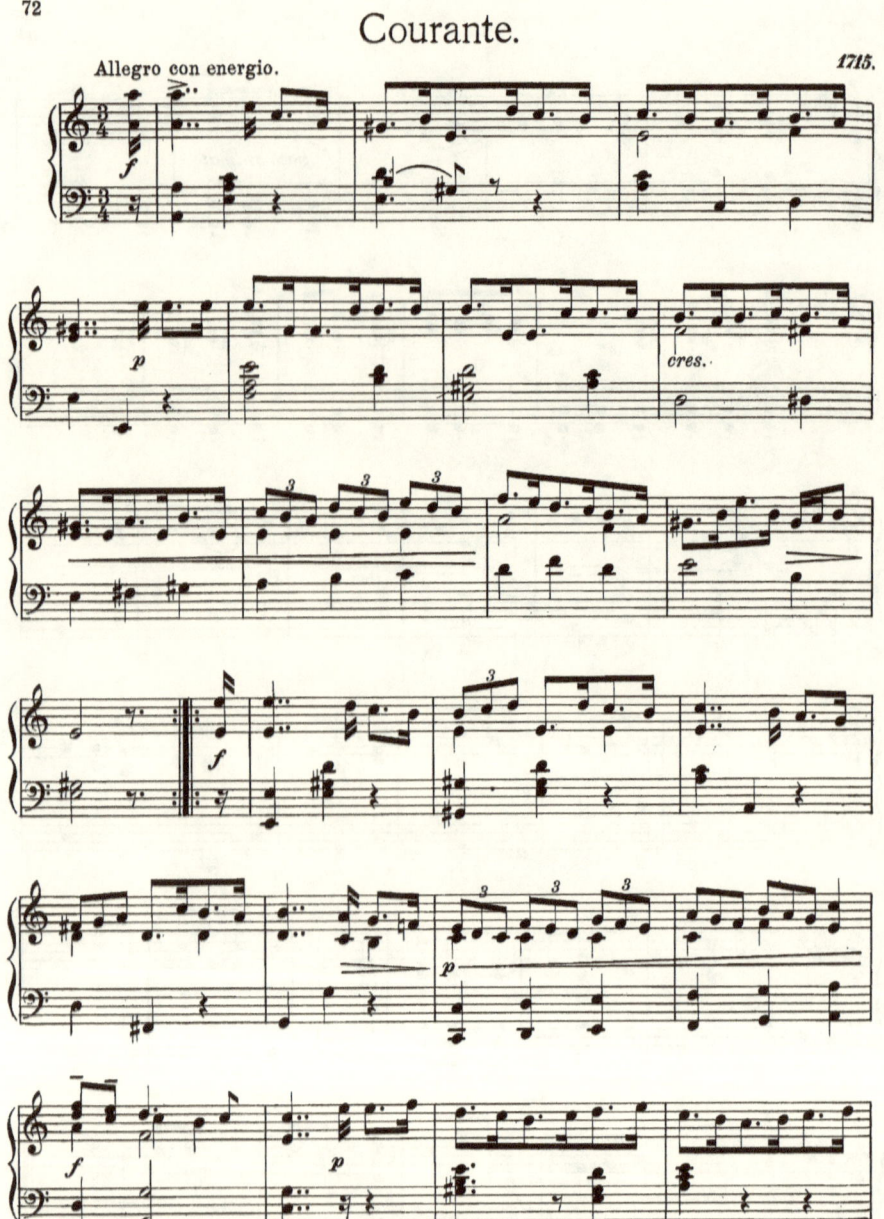

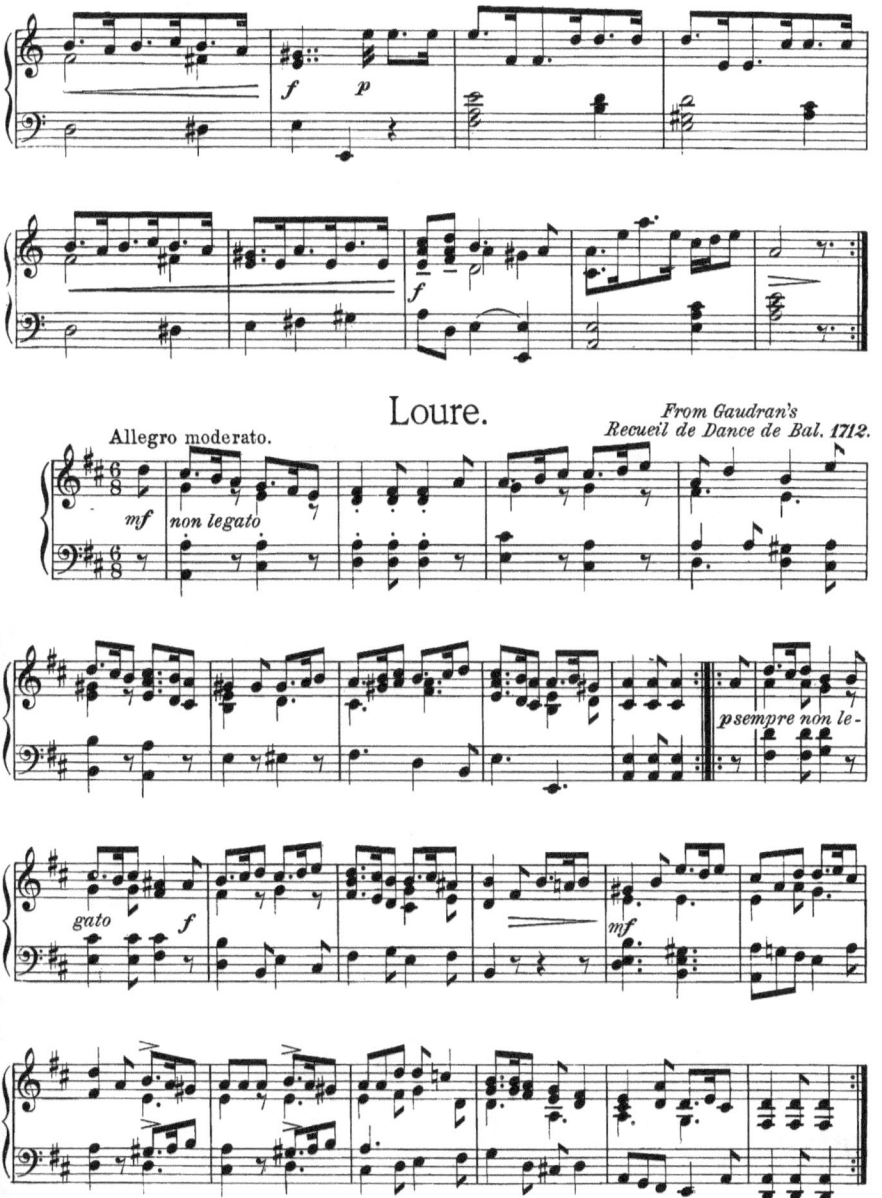

Loure.

From Gaudran's
Recueil de Dance de Bal. **1712.**

Allegro moderato.

mf *non legato*

p sempre non le-

gato *f*

mf

La Chaconne.

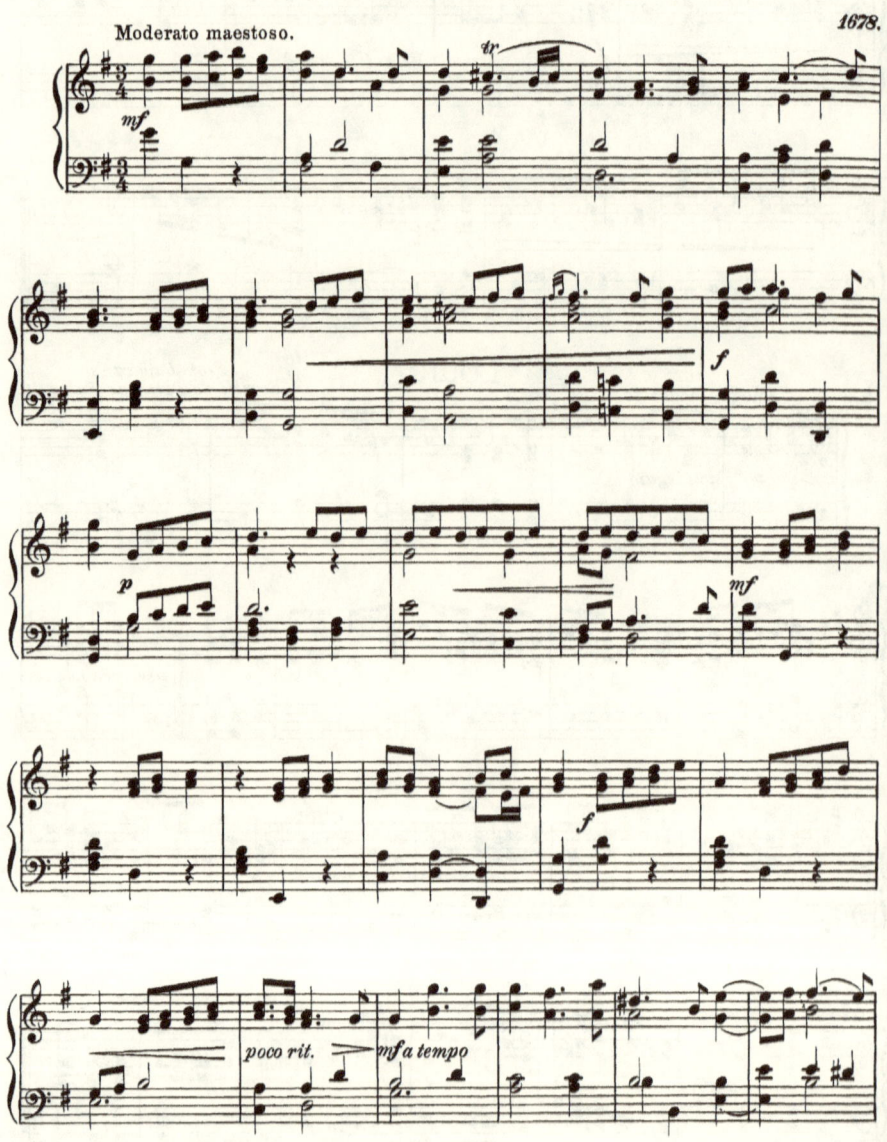

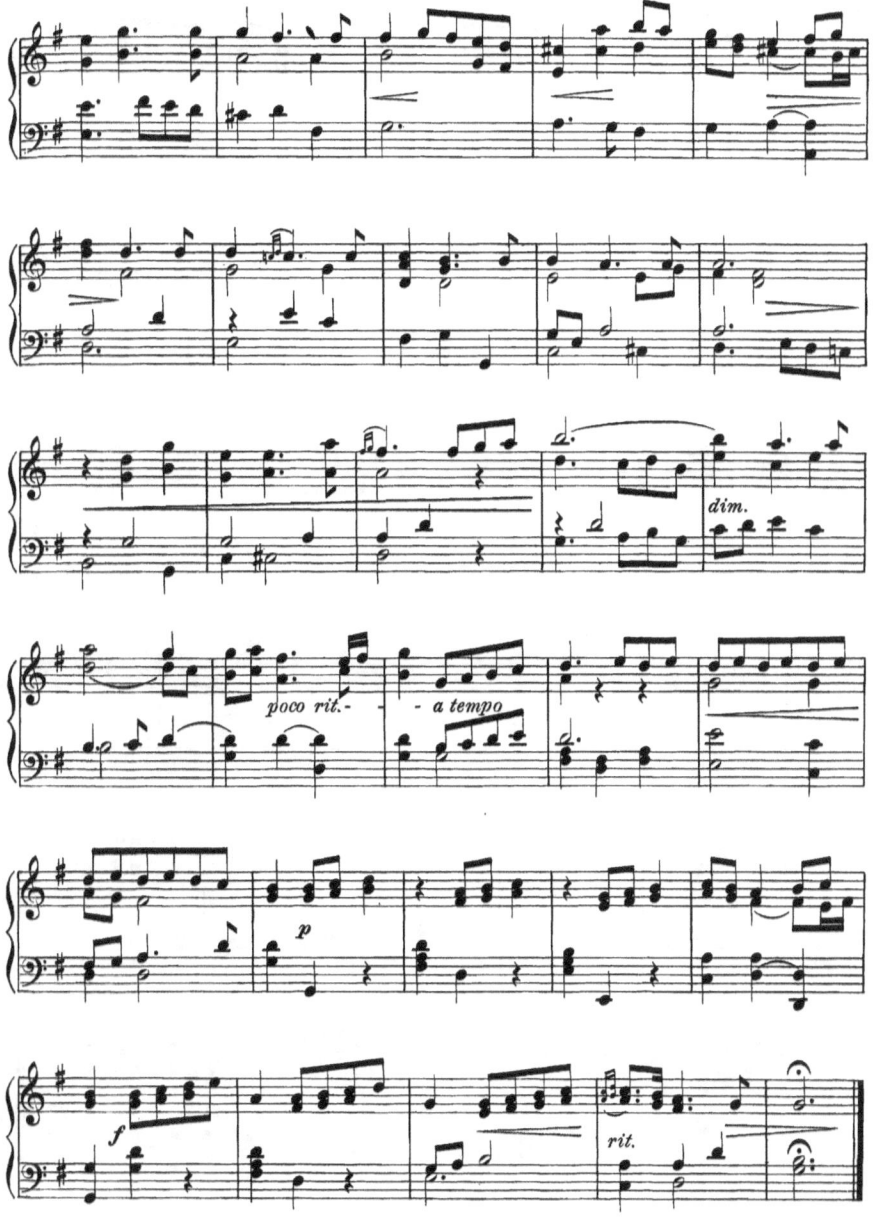

Le Rigaudon.

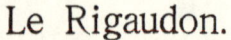

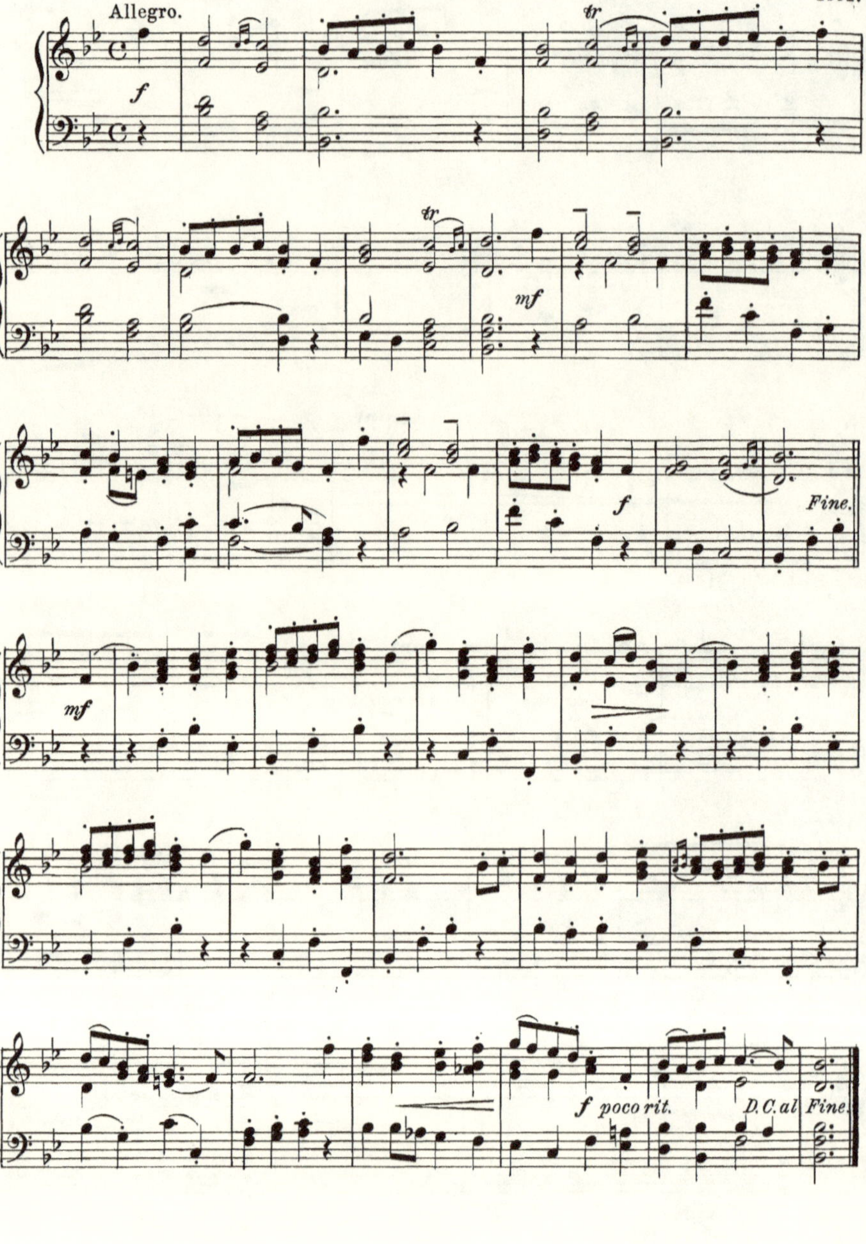

Les Canaries.

From *Gaudran's*
Recueil de Dance de Bal. **1712.**

Andantino con grazia.

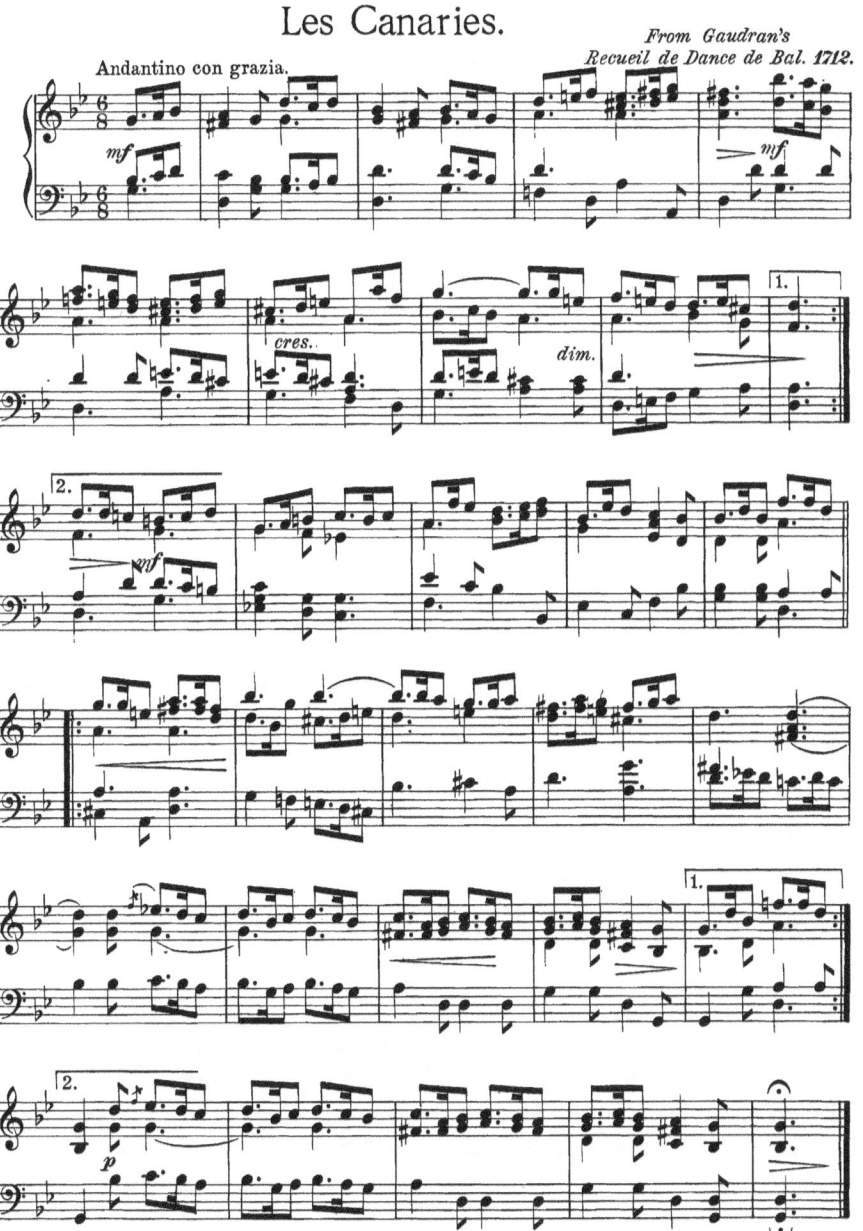

La Forlane.

Allegro con grazia.

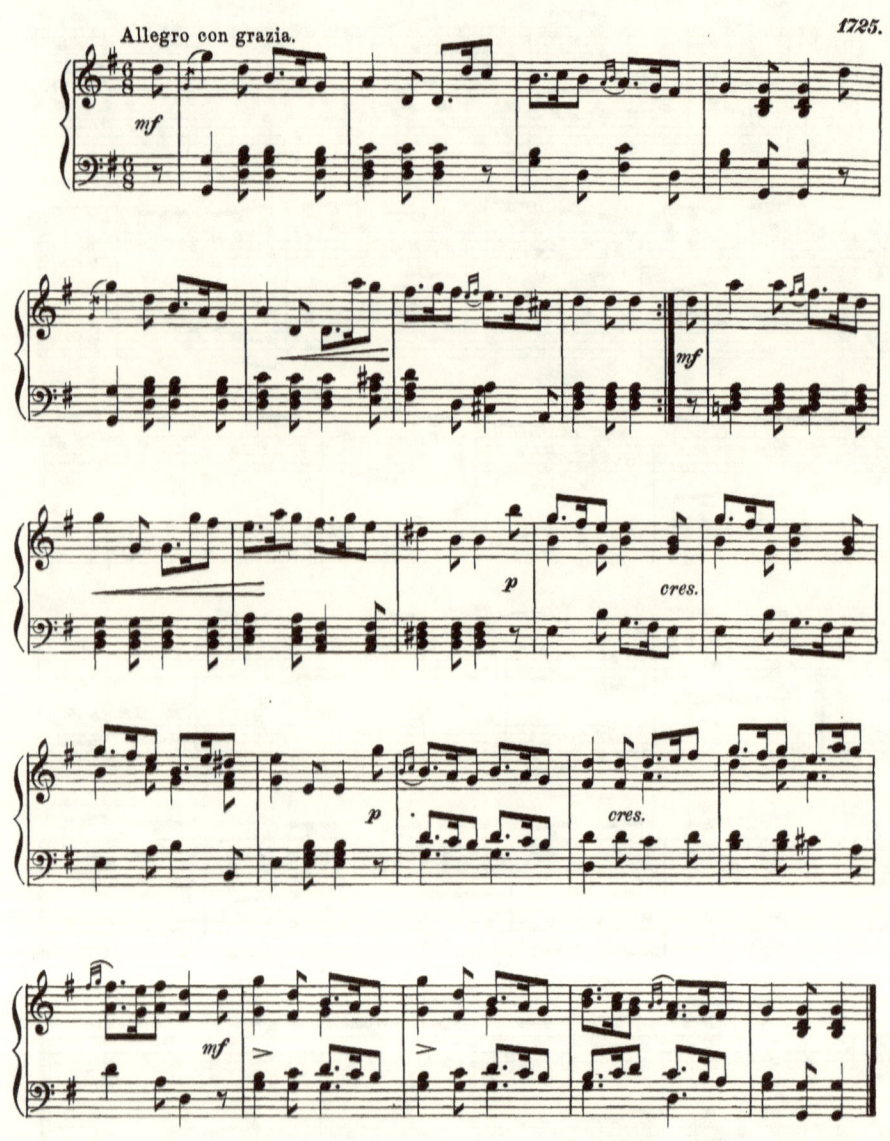

La Musette.

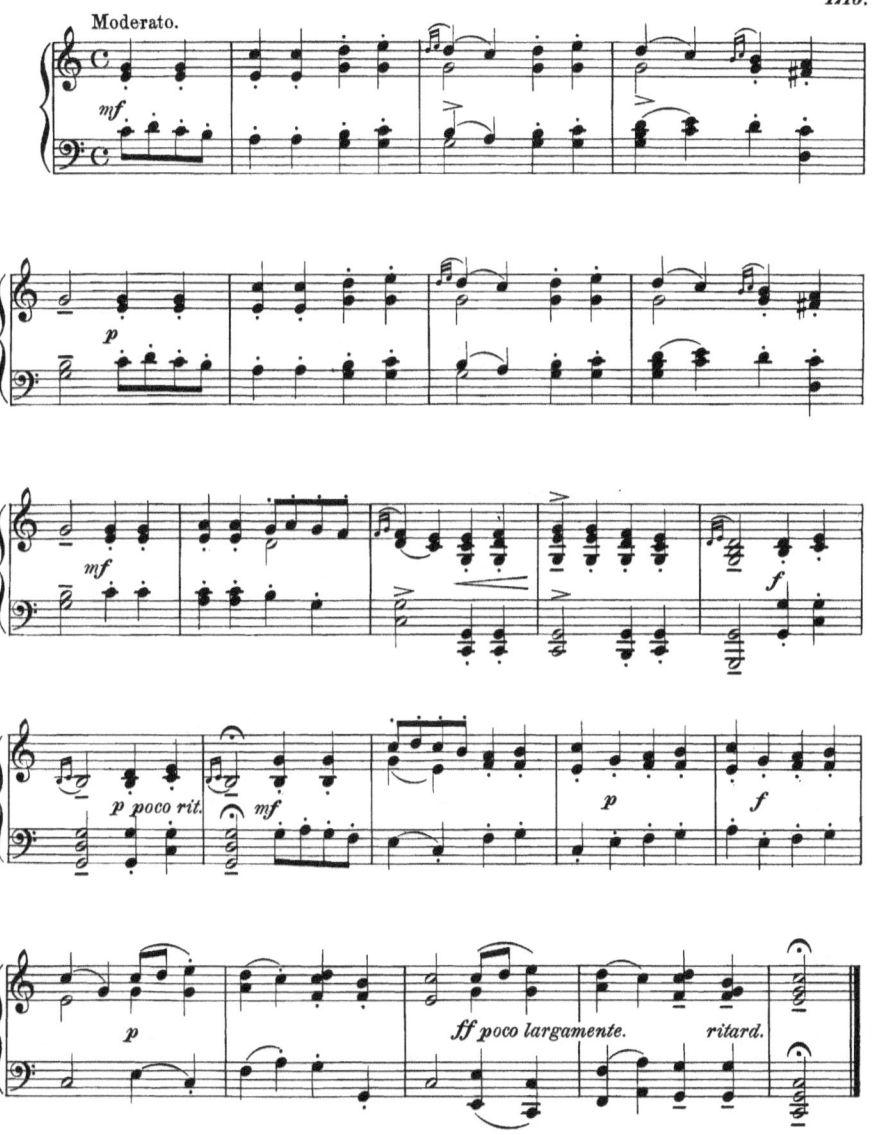

Le Tambourin.

1789.

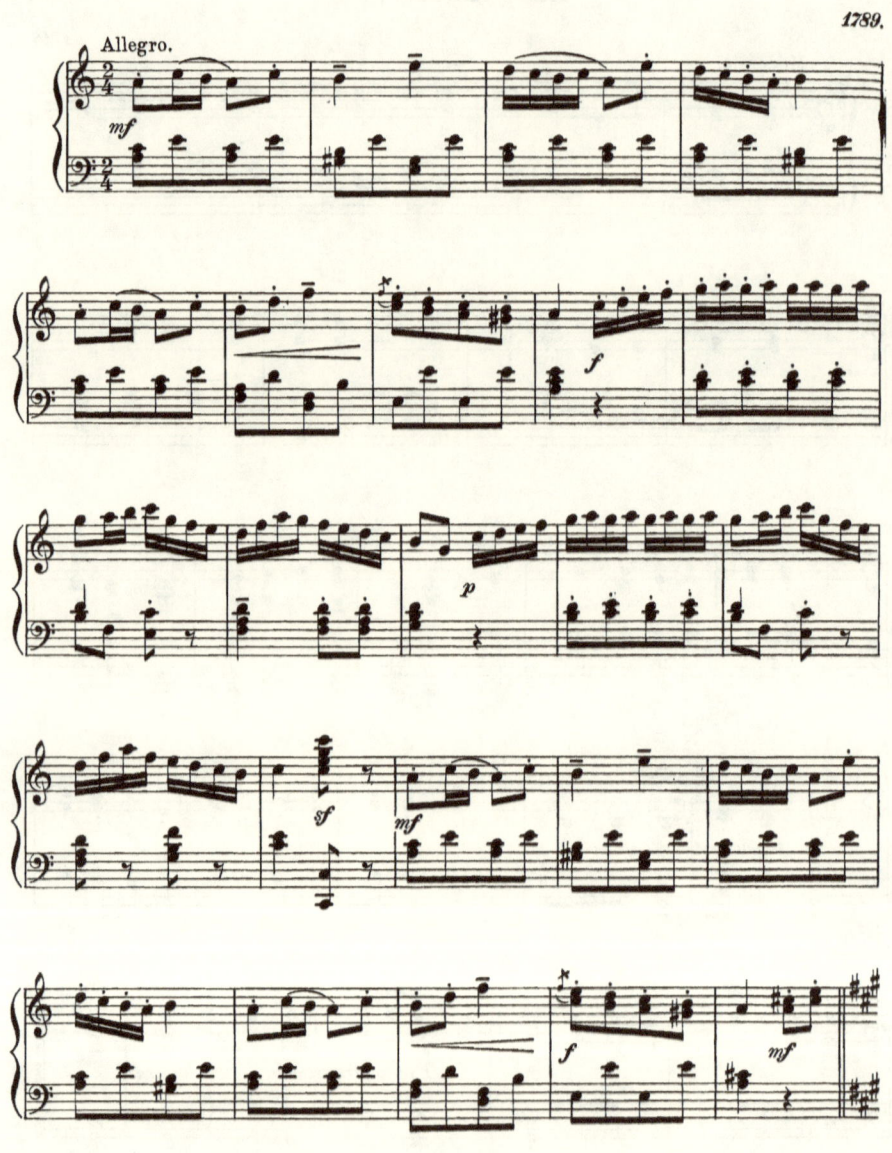

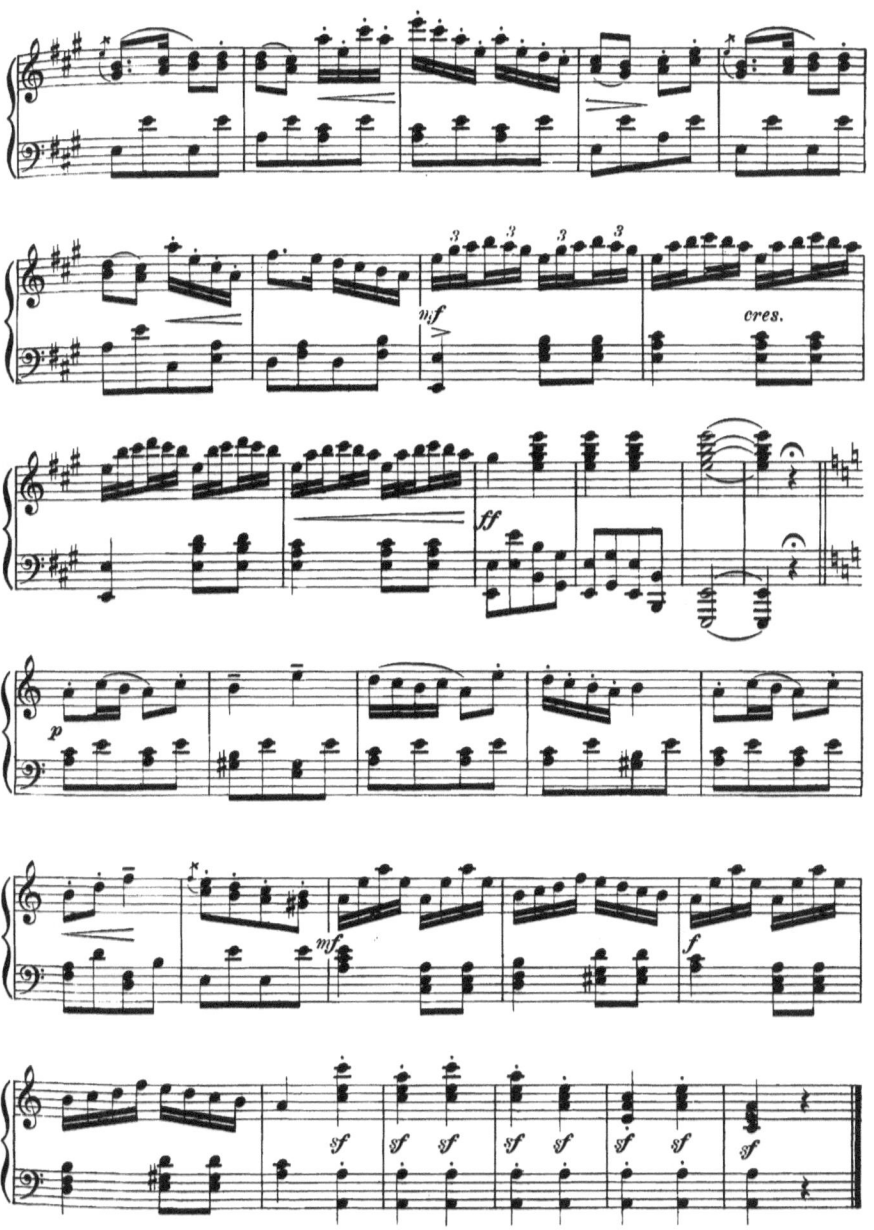